Great Names
in History

ALEXANDER THE GREAT

Great Names in History

356 B.C.—A.D. 1910

By Claud Golding

Essay Index Reprint Series

BOOKS FOR LIBRARIES PRESS
FREEPORT, NEW YORK

First Published 1935
Reprinted 1968

LIBRARY OF CONGRESS CATALOG CARD NUMBER:
68-29206

Preface

GREAT NAMES IN HISTORY needs an explanation.

The articles contained herein are some of those that have appeared daily for the past two years in the London *Evening Standard* under the title of " To-day in History."

Many requests have been made for the publication of the articles in book form, but the problem of including nearly a million words in one volume was insuperable.

It was decided, therefore, to select a sufficient number to fill a book of ordinary size.

The choice has not been easy. There are so many " great names " that might have been included.

The final result is a collection of biographies of characters of various nations, covering a period of more than twenty centuries of the world's history.

The subjects of these biographies include heroes, thinkers, and pioneers in science, industry, and exploration, who have helped to build up the fabric of civilization.

The careers of some will be well known ; others are not so familiar.

In addition to a general outline of a career, less prominent incidents, anecdotes, and controversies are included. Examples are the mystery of Anne Hathaway, the identity of the executioner of Charles I—or was he really beheaded ?—and Alexander the Great's distaste for women.

Contents

7

8   GREAT NAMES IN HISTORY

Illustrations

Great Names in History

I

ALEXANDER THE GREAT, the most eligible
bachelor in the world, disliked women. They
were a torture to the eye, he told the officers of his body-
guard.

As his army subdued one country after another and
his world empire was gradually extending, the most
beautiful women of the conquered territories were
brought captive before him.

But neither the classical features of the Greek beauties,
the languorous glances of the women of the Persian
harem, nor the olive-skinned, almond-eyed coquettes of
his farthest east domains made any impression upon this
impassive adventurer.

Then Roxana came—and conquered.

She was the daughter of Oxyartes, one of the Princes
of Sogdiana, a country near the Persian Gulf which
Alexander invaded in 328 B.C.

Roxana was the fairest maid of all Asia. When
Alexander's victory was celebrated in the usual lavish
style, she, in company with thirty other virgins, danced
before him.

Alexander was in the habit of making up his mind

11

quickly. He gave orders for the wedding to take place immediately, and the ceremony was held according to the ritual of the ancient Iranians.

It may be candidly said that Alexander's summary action was not altogether due to fascination. He himself was regarded as the best-proportioned man of his day, and eugenics may have played a part in his decision, for the Sogdian women were mothers of the bravest offspring.

There was another consideration : it consolidated the conqueror's position as king of Asia.

Biographers of Alexander the Great always become enthusiastic concerning their hero. One of them, Professor F. A. Wright, claims that he is the greatest figure in world-history.

He achieved greater things than Julius Cæsar, was more honourable than Napoleon, and while most of the world-conquerors did nothing to rebuild what they had destroyed, Alexander gave all the conquered nations equal rights with Macedonia.

Alexander was the son of Philip of Macedon. Both his parents were brilliant in intellect, but Alexander surpassed them both, a rather unusual result of such a mating.

Olympias, his mother, lavished all her affection upon her child, probably because of her husband's somewhat loose morals.

At a very early age Alexander had his dreams of conquest, and when he learned of his father's victories complained that there would soon be no territory left for the son to conquer.

There is a tradition that when quite a child Alexander subdued a mad horse. One day the animal was brought to Philip's Court. The King was impressed by its looks, and decided to buy it for £3000, but stipulated a trial ride.

No one, however, was able to mount the animal, and the owner was about to take it away when Alexander remarked that it was a shame to lose such a splendid steed because no one had the courage to manage him.

He mounted, and although the animal was at first restless, he soon had it cantering. When the horse would have stopped, he kept it on the move by digging his heels into the fleshy sides.

About the year 338, Alexander and his father became estranged. It was a clash of two different temperaments ; Alexander being upright and honourable, his father unscrupulous, immoral, and unfaithful to his wife.

When Philip became fascinated with the young and beautiful Cleopatra, daughter of Attalus, one of his trusted commanders, Philip told his wife to leave the court, married his second wife, and held a feast at which every one was drunk.

Attalus stood up and asked the gods to bless the union and to send an heir, whereupon Alexander jumped up and flung a cup of wine into the speaker's face. Immediately there was uproar ; the father tried to kill his son with his sword, but fell helplessly drunk to the floor. Alexander left the chamber remarking, " He wishes to conquer Asia, but cannot stand upon his feet."

Olympias and Alexander left the court and went to live away from trouble. Later Philip asked his son to come back, but it was not long before they were again at loggerheads.

In the meantime Olympias was endeavouring to get her brother to invade Macedonia, but Philip forestalled this by offering his daughter, Cleopatra, to him in marriage.

One day when the festival was being held, Philip was attacked on the way to the theatre and murdered.

Despite opposition, Alexander was proclaimed King

of Macedonia. His first step was to punish all those who had conspired his father's murder, and then he cleared away all opposition by having all claimants to the throne put to death. They included all Philip's illegitimate children, together with Attalus, his daughter Cleopatra, and a child born to her and Philip.

Most of the provinces acknowledged the new king, but some revolted. Greece was troublesome, and Alexander had to take an expeditionary army to subdue the country. On his return he began to prepare for an Asiatic campaign.

In the spring of 334 Alexander crossed the Dardanelles with an army of about 30,000 foot and 5000 horse. The chief horsemen were the Companions, about 2000 strong, divided into eight squadrons, under the command of Philotas. It was the finest fighting force so far produced.

Persia was then the greatest empire in the known world. Alexander defeated the Persians at the battle of Granicus, the headquarters of the Persian Government, and almost all the Grecian cities in the hands of Persia were thus taken over.

Ephesus and Miletus fell, and Halicarnassus surrendered after a siege. An attempt was made to break down the conquests of Alexander by an attack on Greece, but it failed.

Alexander's next objective was the Persians in Syria. Darius III of Persia sent an army, but it was too late, and Alexander entered North Syria, where he found an army commanded by Darius himself. He slipped past them without being observed, and then turned and inflicted upon them a crushing defeat at Issus.

Darius opened negotiations for peace, but Alexander refused. He had determined to conquer the whole of Persia.

Following a seven months' siege, Tyre surrendered,

and its inhabitants were sold into slavery. Then Gaza, too, fell before the Macedonian army, and the way was clear for the conquest of Egypt.

The Egyptians received him as a god who was delivering them from the tyranny of Persia. He stayed in Egypt during the winter of 330-331 B.C., and founded the city of Alexandria. By this time the naval power of Persia was almost broken.

Alexander crossed Syria again, and, making his final arrangements at Tyre, struck straight into the heart of Persia. He found the army of Darius near Nineveh, and at the battle of Arbela, one of the great decisive battles of history, drove before him the Persian army of a million men with his small force of 30,000.

Babylon fell into Alexander's hands, as well as the treasury of the Persian royal house, riches of incalculable value.

Alexander pursued Darius from place to place, and at last reached him near the Caspian Sea ; and here the Persian king was assassinated by his own followers. The crown of Persia was immediately assumed by Bessus, and Alexander had to return to put down the new rebellion.

Alexander was now the king of an immense empire. Whatever country he had visited he had fraternized with the inhabitants, worshipped in Egyptian temples, worn Persian dress, so that he was no longer merely a Macedonian, but a great Oriental despot.

Alexander was having his difficulties. Attempts to overthrow him were made, and a conspiracy had to be put down ruthlessly.

In 327 B.C. he began his march on India, reached the Indus, and then entered Punjab. He had reached the Ganges when a rebellion in the Macedonian army reached an alarming stage.

The soldiers refused to go any farther, and Alexander

began his march westward. The return from India was full of hardships, but reaching home he turned his attention to a reorganization of the country.

He had planned another campaign in Babylonia, when he suddenly became ill with fever. Ten days afterwards, on June 13, 323 B.C., he died.

Arian writes of the last scenes thus :

> The soldiers yearned to set eyes upon him, some that they might see him while he was still alive, others because the news was getting about already that he was no more. Alexander lay speechless as the army defiled before his bed, but he greeted individual soldiers, lifting up his head with difficulty, and making signs to them with his eyes.

The body was embalmed for burial and the army was anxious that it should be interred in Macedonian soil. For more than a year it remained at Babylon, and then as Ptolemy of Egypt had spread a report that the dead Alexander had wished to be buried in the Ammon oasis, the funeral procession took the road to Egypt instead of Macedonia, and the body was finally placed in the Mausoleum at Alexandria.

JULIUS CÆSAR LANDS—AND FALLS

> Caius Julius Cæsar, Consul. We refuse to pay tribute to Rome. We would not submit to the invasion of the gods, much less the Romans, who are but men.

WHEN Julius Cæsar received a defiant message to this effect from Caswallon (or Cassivelaunus), the British chieftain, he rent his clothes.

Having subdued Gaul, Cæsar thought that the island of Britannia would offer no difficulty.

But the Britons had imprisoned his messenger, Comius of Arras. They released him only to carry to his master the decision that they would not recognize his authority.

The sequel was the appearance of a Roman fleet off the shores of Britain in August, 55 B.C.

On the night of the 25th it crossed the Channel in two sections.

At dawn the first section, with Cæsar himself, was in sight of the cliffs of Dover.

A landing would be difficult. They bristled with formidable implements of war.

Cæsar anchored for five hours. A council of war was held. It was at last decided to attempt a landing farther up the Kent coast, near Sandwich.

The Britons followed along the coast in their chariots.

The water was too shallow for some of the ships of

heavy draught. The soldiers were ordered into the lighter vessels of the Roman fleet.

They jumped into the sea. But while Cæsar was trying to assemble them into battle order the Britons attacked " where the ninth wave broke."

The Romans were driven back to their ships.

They clambered aboard. The " barbarians " were forced back by the engines of destruction on the Roman vessels.

The legionaries of Rome did not relish their task. Though most of them had been with the armies that had subdued Gaul, the new foe with their chariots were a different proposition.

At last one legionary jumped from the deck of his ship into the sea. It was the standard-bearer of the tenth Legion.

" Follow me ! " he shouted. With the Eagle aloft he began to wade towards the shore.

Thousands followed his example, despite a hail of stones from the Britons.

They were formed in companies, and the advance began.

Plutarch tells the story of a soldier named Publius who went to the rescue of some of his officers hard beset by the Britons.

He swam to a rock and thus diverted the attention of the attackers. He lost his shield, and his arm was cut to pieces.

Returning to the ship on which Cæsar was watching the battle, he fell upon his knees and asked for mercy. No Roman was excused the loss of his shield.

He was made a centurion on the spot.

The fight continued. The Romans reached land but were attacked by the British cavalry and decimated.

Reinforcements were ordered. The rest of the Roman ships were denuded of their fighting men.

At night-fall the Romans had established themselves on the beach, but their situation was precarious.

The faster vessels of the fleet were sent out to hurry on the second division, which included cavalry.

Two days later eighteen transports were seen.

In the interval, Comius of Arras, who had made friends on his previous visit with Androgeus, son of the late King Lud, got into touch with that rival of Caswallon.

Cæsar regarded Caswallon as a usurper. In his opinion Androgeus was the lawful ruler. But Caswallon had been elected by the nation, and Androgeus was unpopular.

In return for the deposition of Caswallon, Androgeus agreed to open the gates of Caer Troia (London) to the legions of Rome.

While this plot was thickening a gale arose in the Channel. Many of the Roman ships were smashed to pieces.

Most of the stores were lost. The Kent harvest had been cut and carted by the orders of Caswallon in anticipation of the invasion.

Lying watchful at Canterbury was Caswallon, ready to fall upon the invaders at a favourable opportunity.

Word was brought to the invaders that some miles away there were fields of corn still uncut.

Away went the seventh Legion to cut and collect the food so badly needed.

Crafty Caswallon !

The corn had been left as a lure. When the seventh Legion arrived they were ambushed by the Britons.

Cæsar went to the rescue with the rest of the army. The seventh Legion were hard pressed by the chariots of the Britons, who hurled their javelins into the Roman ranks and did great slaughter.

The Britons were driven back. Re-forming, they advanced on the tenth Legion commanded by the Consul.

The area of the battle became extended. It developed into hundreds of small combats. The chariots of the Britons continued to mow down the Roman legions.

The Roman standard was flung down into the trampled straw. Cæsar, in an attempt to save it, was attacked by Nennius, commander of the British cavalry.

Cæsar lunged with his sword and pierced the shield of his adversary. The press of battle separated the contestants, and Cæsar was left without his sword, which was carried away by Nennius.

Cæsar's enemies at Rome declared that he ran away. That may not be true. Nevertheless, it was a rout.

When the sun went down the Romans were back in their camp, with Caswallon half a mile away.

At dawn the British commander attacked three sides of the enemy's camp. It was the fiercest assault which Caswallon had launched, but the Britons were forced back with heavy loss.

For days there was a lull in the fighting.

Cæsar realized that the problem of subduing Britain would have to wait. A larger army would be necessary.

At dead of night his legions embarked. When morning dawned not a Roman soldier was on British soil.

The Roman army reached Boulogne in the third week of September.

Cæsar's first campaign had been a failure. He returned to Rome to find that his popularity had decreased. Only a further—successful—campaign would restore his power.

He returned next year with an enormous army and,

with the aid of Androgeus, the traitor-prince, he conquered.

It is a decade later—44 B.C. instead of 54.

The great Cæsar is no longer great. Factions are against him. Friends have gone over to enemies, and the diviners have prophesied his death for the Ides of March.

For some time ominous dreams have disturbed his sleep, and the man of iron is afraid.

The Senate were due to meet, but Cæsar gave orders to Mark Antony to dismiss it.

But the plot had been carefully hatched. The crafty conspirators sent a messenger to allay the Consul's fears.

Cæsar, said the messenger, must come to the Senate, for the Senate were prepared " with one voice to honour him with the title of king."

" If anyone go and tell them now," the messenger added, " that they must go home, your enemies will have more against you.

" If you are persuaded this is an unlucky day, you must go and tell them yourself that the business should be put off for another time."

So Cæsar went.

As they passed along to Pompey's Hall, they met the soothsayer who had foretold his death.

" The Ides of March are come," said Cæsar with a laugh.

" Yes, but they have not gone," replied the soothsayer.

Cæsar strode into the Senate and took his seat beneath the statue of Pompey.

There came one with a petition that Cæsar would release his brother from exile. It was Metellus Cimber.

The Consul waved him aside, but Cimber with both hands pulled away Cæsar's gown.

It was the signal.

Casca struck the Consul with his sword. It was a weak blow, delivered half-heartedly.

Cæsar jumped to his feet. Clutching the weapon, he cried, " Villain ! what dost thou mean ? "

" Brother, help ! " shrieked Casca.

The Senate was in an uproar. Loyal members were afraid to go to the Consul's aid, ignorant of the strength of the conspirators.

Swords flashed. A circle of gleaming steel floated within inches of Cæsar's breast.

The wounded Cæsar made a brave show of resistance. Then Brutus stepped forward and struck.

No man had received more honours from the hand of Cæsar than Brutus. He had received a free pardon when he deserved death for treasonable activities against the State, and Cæsar had actually named him for the consulship in preference to Cassius.

" Et tu, Brute ! " Cæsar whispered. " Then fall, Cæsar ! "

Twenty-three wounds were counted in his body.

A procession soon emerged from the Senate House, led by Brutus and the rest of the conspirators. They carried aloft their bloodstained swords, and marched towards the Capitol.

" Liberty ! " they shouted repeatedly, as they passed along the crowded streets.

III

Marcus Aurelius, Stoic-Emperor

MARCUS AURELIUS ANTONINUS, Emperor of Rome, who succeeded on the death of Antoninus Pius, once remarked :

> To the gods I am indebted for having good grandfathers, good parents, a good sister, good teachers, good associates, good kinsmen and friends, nearly everything good.

Perhaps the exception was his wife, Faustina. He does not include her in his eulogy, although she bore him eleven children, and he was content to ignore the rumours which cast a doubt upon her chastity.

She was charged with infidelity by two prominent Romans, but her death was a great shock to the Emperor.

Aurelius was born in Rome, A.D. 121. Originally he was Marcus Annius Verus, his father of Spanish extraction having received patrician rank at the hands of Vespasian.

Marcus was three months old at the death of his father, and he was adopted by his grandfather.

At an early age he attracted the attention of the Emperor Hadrian, and when Hadrian adopted as his successor Titus Antoninus Pius, uncle of Marcus, he stipulated that he should adopt Marcus.

At the age of fifteen Marcus was betrothed to Fabia, the daughter of Aelius Cæsar, but this engagement was broken off by Antoninus Pius, and he was betrothed instead to Faustina, the daughter of Antoninus.

23

In 139 he received the title of Cæsar, and a year later was made consul.

Adopting the severe regimen of the Stoics, he lived so abstemious and laborious a life that his health began to suffer. His Stoic tutors taught him to work hard, to deny himself, to avoid listening to slander, to endure misfortunes, to be kind in correcting others.

During the reign of Antonius Pius (138 to 161) the two were closely associated in the administration of the country, and when Antoninus Pius died he recommended Aurelius as his successor.

He married Faustina about the year 146, and a daughter was born.

Aurelius was reluctant to rule alone, and therefore invited another adopted son of Antoninus to share the responsibility. This was the first time that Rome had two emperors in close association.

Verus, his colleague, however, was a weak, self-indulgent man. In the first year of his reign Aurelius's wife gave birth to twins, one of whom was later the Emperor Commodus.

Aurelius had not held the reins of government for more than a short space when troubles began. The Tiber overflowed and swept away a large portion of Rome.

Fields were flooded, and thousands of cattle drowned. This caused a disastrous famine.

On top of this followed earthquakes, fires, and plagues of insects.

In Britain there was an insurrection and an attempt to induce the general Statius Priscus to proclaim himself emperor, while the Parthians began an attack on Cappadocia, annihilated the Roman forces there, and overran Syria.

Verus, the associate Emperor, was sent to deal with

the Parthians. Usually a man of great courage, he fell into sensual excesses. But for his having competent generals it is probable that Rome itself would have fallen.

Eventually the Parthians were beaten, but the succession of disasters so preyed upon the minds of the Roman people that it was freely believed that the days of Rome were numbered.

Still there was no tranquillity ; the Parthians were giving anxiety, the Britons were revolting, and the barbarians beyond the Alps were preparing for an onslaught upon Rome.

Most of the time of Aurelius was taken up with trying to straighten out the tangle to which he had succeeded.

He himself went to the wars, and for a year fought the barbarians, who eventually sued for peace.

In 169 Verus died, and there were many who declared that Aurelius had poisoned him, although there is good reason to believe that he died of apoplexy.

F. W. Farrar, in *Seekers after God*, gives a glowing account of Aurelius as sole ruler of Rome :

> He regarded himself as being, in fact, the servant of all. The registry of the citizens, the suppression of litigation, the elevation of public morals, the care of minors, the retrenchment of public expenses, the limitation of gladiatorial games and shows, the care of roads, the restoration of senatorial privileges, the appointment of none but worthy magistrates, even the regulation of street traffic, these and numberless other duties so completely absorbed his attention, that, in spite of indifferent health, they often kept him at severe labour from early morning till long after midnight. His position, indeed, often necessitated his presence at games and shows, but on these occasions he occupied himself either in reading, in being read to, or in writing notes. He was one of those who held that nothing should be done hastily, and that few crimes were worse than the waste of time.

Other matters that received his attention were lega and judicial reforms and the falling birth-rate.

For three years from 169 Aurelius was compelled to live at Carnuntum while prosecuting a war against two German tribes, who were eventually driven across the Danube.

The way in which one of the marauding tribes, the Quadi, was beaten in 174 was regarded as a miracle.

The story is told that the Romans, caught in a ravine, were suffering from thirst. Then came a sudden storm with abundance of rain and thunder and lightning.

While the rain relieved the thirst of the Romans, the thunder startled the Quadi to such an extent that the Romans were able to gain a complete victory.

The triumph was called long afterwards " The Miracle of the Thundering Legion," and the victory was attributed by the pagan writers to the magic of an Egyptian, called Arnuphis, who called upon Mercury to lend his aid, while the Christians had a different interpretation, and ascribed the victory to the prayers of the soldiers.

Aurelius was fighting in Germany when news was brought that Avidius Cassius, the Roman commander in Asia, had revolted and proclaimed himself emperor. Three months later the revolutionary was murdered, how, or by whom, is not known.

It was naturally suggested that Aurelius had had a hand in the assassination, but his subsequent actions do not support this, for he had no difficulty in bringing about peace in the provinces that had revolted, and treated them with extraordinary leniency.

When the letters of Cassius were brought to him, he threw them into the fire without reading them.

While he was restoring order in the affected provinces his wife Faustina died.

To what extent Aurelius was concerned in the persecution of Christians during his reign is doubtful. There is no doubt that the persecution reached as great a severity at this time as at any other period of Pagan Rome, and there has been much controversy on the point.

Finally, Aurelius was called again to Germany to carry on the war, and after a series of successes, according to some authorities, fell ill of a strange disease which caused his death after seven days, on March 17, 180, in the fifty-ninth year of his age.

Other authorities declare that he was poisoned at the instance of Commodus, while others affirm that he died of a disease of the stomach. Commodus was with his father when he died, and was instrumental in the erection of the Antonine Column to his father's memory.

This column, which is now in the Piazza Colonna at Rome, has sculpture in relief around the base depicting the miracle of the Thundering Legion and the victories of Aurelius.

It is probable that during the reign of Marcus Aurelius a retrogade movement against the supremacy of Rome set in in Britain.

No relics or inscriptions have been found north of Hadrian's wall which relate to emperors after Marcus Aurelius, although there are many which concern his predecessor Antoninus Pius, and there is reason to believe that the Romans lost a great part of the Lowlands of Scotland about this time.

IV

St Augustine, First Archbishop of Canterbury

THE market-place in Rome was crowded with sightseers.

When the galleys arrived with their strange cargo of slaves the news quickly spread, and citizens turned out in their thousands to gaze curiously at that motley crowd of Nubians, Greeks, Syrians, Egyptians, and other nationalities, who were to be sold to the highest bidders.

The scantily-clad negroes shivered, but grinned inanely under the searching glances of would-be buyers.

The Greeks, sour-faced with cunning eyes, apprehensive as to the result of the sale, shrank behind the others, especially conscious of their position, for Greece had once been the mistress of the world.

Among the collection were three youths whose fair skin and golden hair brought sympathy from the onlookers.

They contrasted oddly with their fellows ; their blue eyes were clear, innocent, and wondering.

There was movement in the crowd as some one fought his way gradually through the throng. It was the monk Gregory, who was attracted by the strange apparition of the blond slaves.

He inquired whence the strange but beautiful children had been brought.

" From Britain, where the inhabitants are as fair as they," was the reply.

SAINT AUGUSTINE
Royal MS., British Museum

" Do they worship the one God ? " he asked.

" Nay," was the answer.   " Alas ! they are pagans."

" Ah," sighed Gregory, " more is the pity that faces so full of light and brightness should be in the hands of the Prince of Darkness.   Alas ! that such grace of out-ward appearance should accompany minds without the grace of God within."

Then, upon being told that the youths were of the race of Angles or English, he remarked, " Well, rightly are they called Angles, for they have the faces of angels, and they ought to be fellow-heirs of heaven."

From further inquiries Gregory learned that the children had come from the land of Deira (wild deer), the name which then belonged to the country between the rivers Tyne and Humber.

" What is the name of the King of that country," he asked, and on being told that it was Ella, he exclaimed : " Allelujah !   The praise of God, their Creator, shall be sung in those parts."

From the market-place Gregory went to the palace of the Pope and pleaded to be allowed to preach the Gospel to the English people.

The request was granted, and Gregory, with several companions, sailed for Britain.   But the legend records that, on the third day of their journey, as they rested from the rays of the midday sun, a locust settled upon the book that Gregory was reading.

Here was an omen, thought the monk.   Solemnly he said to his companions : " Rightly is it called *locusta*, because it seems to say to us *loco sta*—stay in your place.

" I see that we shall not be able to finish our journey."

He had barely spoken when couriers arrived recalling him to Rome, where the citizens were clamouring for his return.

There is more fiction than fact in this story, but that

there is a foundation of truth in it is shown in Gregory's anxiety to convert Britain.

When years had passed away and he had become Pope, he remembered the " pagan " people of the country which the Romans had attempted to colonize.

He awaited the right moment, and when he learned that one of the Saxon kings had married a Christian princess, he gauged that the time had arrived.

From the monastery on the Mount of Coelian he chose Augustine and forty of his monks for a missionary campaign in England.

In that country, Ethelbert was king of Kent, with influence over the other Saxon kings as far north as the Humber.

Ethelbert was a pagan, but his wife, Bertha, was a Christian. She had married on the understanding that she should be allowed to pursue her own religion.

In a small chapel outside Canterbury she and her chaplain, a French Bishop, worshipped.

The story of St Augustine, first Archbishop of Canterbury, presupposes a pagan Britain, but this can hardly be true, for there is evidence of churches having existed in England before his time.

When Augustine and his followers landed they had an agreeable surprise, for Ethelbert received them more or less graciously.

They were allowed to live in the island of Thanet, and later in Ethelbert's capital of Canterbury.

Ethelbert was baptized, and his example was followed shortly afterwards by many of his leading subjects. Augustine was given permission to preach all over the country, while the King laid down that no sort of compulsion should be used for the conversion of the people.

In Rome the Pope watched closely the events in England, and when Augustine had established himself he was recalled to Arles and consecrated bishop of the English.

It had been the intention of the Pope to divide England into twenty-four dioceses, under archbishops at London and York, but Canterbury was substituted for London out of respect for King Ethelbert, who now was a keen supporter of the Faith.

Augustine's success in this country was due in great measure to the permission of Gregory for the missionary to adopt from the usage of other churches, " whatever should prove pleasing to God."

Thus in the teaching which he gave to the English Augustine was careful to allow some of the form and ceremony of the religion of the English people to remain.

On the other hand, when he was made Archbishop of Canterbury, he reigned in true pontifical authority. He made an effort to come to an arrangement with the Welsh Church, and he met the Welsh bishops at Malmesbury.

The failure to come to an agreement was due to detail rather than important matters of doctrine. The Welsh objected to the observance of Easter on the day appointed by Rome, and such-like unessentials.

In 604 Augustine consecrated Mellitus Bishop of London, and Justus Bishop of Rochester. After naming Laurence as his successor, he died on May 26, 607, and was buried at Canterbury in the Church of St Peter and St Paul, afterwards called St Augustine's Abbey, which King Ethelbert had founded.

Ethelbert also assisted in building a cathedral church at Canterbury, " in the name of our Holy Saviour, God and Lord Jesus Christ," whither the body of St Augustine was taken in 1091.

V

THE "HAMMER" OF THE SCOTTISH NATION

EDWARD I was one of the ablest of English sovereigns, but there are indelible blots on his memory.

He was a great military leader, but the brilliance of his victories was dulled by his vindictiveness.

As a Prince he achieved great feats of arms in the Holy Land, but when he took Nazareth he cruelly massacred the Turks.

During his reign the Jews were banished from the country. Having robbed them of their possessions, he proceeded to annex to the Crown the estates of his nobles, until one of them, the powerful Earl Warrene, put a stop to his depredations.

Warrene was asked to produce the titles to his property. He immediately drew his sword and said : " By this instrument do I hold my lands, and by the same do I intend to defend them."

Edward was angered when King Llewelyn of Wales did not think it of sufficient moment to attend Edward's coronation. Edward thereupon requested him to come to London to pay homage. At the same time he seized the Welsh king's bride, the daughter of the dead Earl of Leicester.

Llewelyn asked for a guarantee of safe conduct and the release of his bride.

The English king refused, and immediately began an attack on Wales. The Welsh king was excommunicated by the Archbishops of Canterbury and York, and the English Parliament pronounced judgment against him.

Wales was invaded and Llewelyn's army driven into the fastnesses of the mountains. The Welsh king submitted, but his brother David persuaded him to carry on the conflict. Edward sent the Cinque Ports fleet to Anglesey, captured it, and then prepared to attack Llewelyn in the mountains.

He flung a bridge of boats across the Menai Straits and tried to cross with his army, to find that Llewelyn had the bridge covered.

With the aid of a traitorous Welshman the English army crossed by an unknown ford and approached the Welsh at the rear.

In the meantime Llewelyn had left his stronghold to reconnoitre. He saw the English approaching and tried to return, when he was accosted by an English noble, the Earl of Mortimer, who advanced upon him, perceiving him to be a Welshman, but unaware of his identity.

Although lightly armed the King did not attempt to avoid the fight. At the end of the encounter the last King of Wales lay dead.

The Welsh awaited the return of their sovereign in vain. The English banners began to wave upon their heights. They found themselves attacked on all sides.

Those who escaped the swords of the English fled in hopeless confusion, and Wales was annexed to the English Crown with a facility that surprised Edward.

After the battle, Mortimer and several knights went to the spot where he had fought the Welshman. The dead man was recognized.

Mortimer cut off Llewelyn's head and carried it to Edward, who sent it up to London, adorned with a silver crown. It was exhibited in Cheapside, and was placed afterwards on a spike at the Tower of London.

3

The heart and bowels were burned, and the four quarters of the body were exposed at Bristol, Northampton, York, and Winchester.

Scotland was Edward's next objective.

Alexander III of Scotland died, leaving as heir his grand-daughter Margaret, then in Norway and about three years of age. But she died on the way to Scotland.

Thirteen men laid claim to the Crown of Scotland, the chief competitors being Baliol and Robert Bruce. Edward was invited by one of the regents to go and settle the problem.

He demanded a recognition of his sovereignty over Scotland. The Scots were astonished, and asked for time for deliberation.

Eventually they agreed, and Baliol was given the Crown of Scotland by Edward.

Four years later Baliol revolted, and Edward neglected his war with France and turned upon Scotland. He took Berwick by storm and put its garrison to death. The Scots were badly equipped and were heavily defeated in every battle.

Gradually the Scottish castles surrendered, and Baliol, divested of his kingly robes, performed penance and resigned his kingdom.

It was at this period of Scotland's misfortunes that William Wallace arose.

Led by Wallace the Scots flew to arms, and for a time they were successful. The English were expelled from the country, and the Scotsmen crossed the border. Edward was in Flanders, but quickly hurried home, and at the head of 80,000 infantry and 7000 cavalry crossed into Scotland.

At Linlithgow in the dead of night Edward's horse took fright and kicked him in the ribs as he slept. Two ribs were broken.

Edward reassured his troops, and in the morning mounted his horse.

The army marched to Falkirk. Here the forces met.

For a time fortune favoured the Scots. Then the tide turned. The Scottish troops fled and left 20,000 dead.

One by one the Scottish castles submitted, and Wallace was captured. He was brought to Westminster and arraigned as a traitor. He declared he had never sworn allegiance to Edward, but the judges decided against him, and he was found guilty of treason.

He was hanged, drawn, and quartered. His head was exposed on London Bridge, and his limbs were sent back to Scotland.

But Scotland was not yet beaten. A new insurrection broke out under Robert Bruce.

Edward went north with an army, but fell ill on the way. He reached the village of Burgh-on-Sands, on the shores of the Solway Firth, and there he died on July 7, 1307, at the age of sixty-eight.

His body was brought to London and buried at Westminster Abbey.

On the tomb was placed the inscription in Latin :

" Here lies Edward the First, the Hammer of the Scottish Nation."

VI

SIR WILLIAM WALLACE, SCOTTISH PATRIOT AND MARTYR

THERE was a sensational prelude to the Bartholomew Fair of 1305.

All the citizens of London gathered to witness a drama which they had anticipated with satisfaction for some days.

It was the execution of Sir William Wallace, the Scottish patriot.

They had been made to believe that Wallace was the devil incarnate.

They had not been told that Wallace had fought valiantly against the rapacity of Edward I of England.

The treatment of the Scotsman by orders of the King is an indelible blot on that monarch's memory.

At Westminster Hall they had mocked Wallace with a crown of laurel when charging him with being a traitor and with having burned villages and abbeys, destroyed castles, and slain the liege subjects of his master the King.

To this charge Wallace replied that he had never taken an oath of allegiance to the King. He had fought against the subjects of Edward because they had oppressed his country.

He was condemned to death as a matter of course.

In the middle of last century a document was discovered in the MSS at the British Museum which gives a record of the exploits of Wallace.

It relates that John Baliol forfeited the crown of

Scotland, and Edward conquered the country. The King received the fealty and homage of the " prelates, earls, barons, and others."

Edward arranged a system of Government " according to the laws and customs of that land."

William Wallace raised a large body of followers and attacked the English officers. He slew William de Hezelrig, sheriff of Lanark, whose body he afterwards cut to pieces.

He stormed the English garrisons and caused his writs to extend all through Scotland, " as if he were superior lord of that realm."

He summoned Parliaments, attempted to ally himself with the King of France, ravaged Northumberland, Cumberland, and Westmorland, fought against the King, and refused to accept a treaty of peace when it was offered to him.

On the day before St Bartholomew, Wallace, in heavy chains, was dragged by horses through the streets from the Tower to Smithfield, followed by a howling crowd.

Smithfield in those days was a recreation ground for London. There youths played football, and elderly men played bowls. The upper classes had a galloping ground where they exercised their horses.

A fair was held there during St Bartholomew-tide.

When the time for Wallace's execution arrived the youths deserted their football and the old men their bowls. The merry-making ceased.

Wallace submitted without a murmur. He merely asked that a book of Psalms might be placed in his hand. This had been taken from him at his arrest.

He handed the book to a priest and asked him to hold it open before his eyes.

When life had left him, his head was struck off, and his body was divided in quarters.

The head was placed on London Bridge, and the limbs were exhibited at Newcastle, Berwick, Perth, and Stirling.

Hatred of the English had been implanted at an early age in Wallace's mind.

His father and his elder brother were slain. His uncle, a priest, fostered the lad's desire for revenge.

It is said that Wallace was outlawed when young for killing the son of the English governor of Dundee, who had insulted him.

He was about twenty-seven when he was involved in a quarrel with English officers in Lanark. He escaped to Cartland Crags, a rugged glen near the town.

Hezelrig, the English sheriff, put Wallace's wife and servants to death and burned his house.

A little band of determined men gathered around Wallace. They raided the home of Hezelrig, slaughtered him, and cut up his body.

Thenceforth Wallace carried on a guerilla warfare against the English.

Isolated parties of the enemy were surprised. Their provisions were taken and they were killed. Wallace then retreated to fastnesses into which the English could not follow.

Wallace's exploits aroused the Scottish nobles. Sir William Douglas captured the castles of Durisdeer and Sanquhar. Then Wallace and Douglas joined forces and marched westward, capturing every fortress on the way.

Edward I was alarmed.

He sent an army of 40,000 to crush the insurrection.

Many other nobles joined Wallace's standard, but dissensions arose.

When they could not oppose a united front to Edward's army, Douglas, Robert Bruce, and others made their submission to Edward.

Wallace and Sir Andrew Moray moved north, capturing more castles.

A powerful army under the Earl of Surrey and Cressingham, the Scottish Treasurer, set out for Stirling.

In the battle that followed, the English were routed by the better strategy of Wallace.

The Treasurer, Cressingham, and over 5000 men fell in the fight.

Dundee surrendered. Other strongholds of the English were subdued.

Wallace took over the government of the kingdom and tried to alleviate the sufferings of the people. Famine and pestilence were reducing the population.

He determined on a raid into England. He crossed the Border at the head of a small force, and turned Northumberland and Cumberland into a wilderness.

With enormous booty he returned to Scotland to feed his starving countrymen.

At an assembly of the principal noblemen of the country, Wallace was chosen Regent of Scotland.

In the summer of 1298, Edward invaded Scotland with an army of nearly 100,000.

As the result of the treachery of two Scottish nobles, Wallace was defeated and his army was scattered.

He went to France to obtain aid from the French king. It was the wrong time. Philip had concluded a treaty with Edward and had agreed to marry his sister to the English king.

Wallace was arrested at Amiens and thrown into prison. Later he was released. He returned to Scotland.

In the meantime Edward had beaten the Scots.

Wallace was outlawed, and a price was set upon his head. Betrayed by Sir John Monteith, a Scottish baron, the patriot was captured in the mountains and brought to England.

VII

"Good King Robert" of Scotland

And ages after he was laid in earth,
"The Good King Robert" was the name he bore.

ASK a Scotsman the name of his national hero and he will most probably declare for Robert Bruce, the restorer of Scottish independence.

At the time of his death—rather untimely because of the strenuous life he had led—all classes made " great lamentation over his decease, and strong, bearded men wept full sore, regretting his worthy bounty, his wit, his strength, his bravery and, above all, his kindness and courtesy."

Bruce broke the English yoke at the Battle of Bannockburn, after nine years of continuous fighting with the legions of Edward I and Edward II.

At times he had been a fugitive from the army of Edward I, and he and a small party of followers had had to seek safety in the mountains.

While he was hiding from his enemies in an old shed he saw the spider endeavouring to spin its web. Six times the gossamer thread broke. At the seventh time it succeeded in laying the base for its web.

So Robert Bruce went forth encouraged by the little spider.

Before the end of the reign of old Edward I the English hold upon Scotland was already loosening. With the accession of the second Edward, a weakling unfit to govern, Bruce's opportunity arrived.

Edward II had neither the ability nor inclination to carry on the Scottish war. Several times he crossed the border half-heartedly in attempts to regain lost territory.

Once he spent three weeks in Ayrshire, but returned to England without having achieved anything of importance.

Then the English king sent the Earl of Richmond into Scotland at the head of a powerful army. Bruce prudently retreated to the north of Scotland ; but soon afterwards fell upon Richmond unawares and defeated him with great slaughter.

The citizens of Aberdeen rallied to the Scottish banner, and storming the castle of that town, Bruce soon reduced the stronghold.

Successes now came one after the other, until only one castle of importance was holding out.

Besieged in Stirling Castle, Sir Philip Mowbray, the English Governor, made a brave defence. But provisions ran short, and he had no option but to sue for a truce.

There followed one of the most amazing arrangements ever entered into by two enemy commanders. Mowbray offered to surrender the fortress if not relieved before the feast of St John the Baptist—June 24—in the following year.

It was an absurd proposal, to which Robert Bruce would never have consented, but his brother, Edward, who was making the assault on the castle, agreed to the one-sided truce.

Robert Bruce was annoyed. Having found previously that the English were not too squeamish about keeping engagements, he could have repudiated the terms of the agreement.

But he went one better than his brother, and allowed Mowbray to go to London to advise Edward of the precarious situation at Stirling.

For once, Edward showed a little enterprise. He made immense preparations for the relief of Stirling Castle.

The whole military forces of England were assembled at Berwick on June 11, 1314, reinforced by troops from Ireland, and a powerfully equipped fleet carrying supplies.

It was the most magnificent army that England had ever produced. It amounted to 100,000 men, with 50,000 archers and 40,000 cavalry.

Eleven days later Edward crossed the border at its head and marched upon Stirling. Bruce, with his 30,000, including 500 cavalry, arranged his army in line, or squares, or circles, according to the nature of the ground.

It was similar strategy to that which was employed by Wellington at Waterloo.

Bruce's position was about two miles from Stirling, and he was protected on each flank by natural or artificial defences.

On his right wing were the steep and rugged banks of the River Bannockburn, beyond which was a bog.

In front of him was a bottle-neck through which only a restricted number of English could attack at one time.

On June 23 the English army was seen approaching, a panorama of colour, with banners flying and armour sparkling in the sunlight.

The English king ordered Sir Robert Clifford to attack on the left flank of the enemy with 800 picked horsemen. They were met with 500 Scottish cavalry and forced to retreat.

King Robert could be seen riding along the front of his line on a small charger, clad in armour and carrying a battle-axe.

He was easily recognizable by the golden coronet which he wore on his helmet. Sir Henry de Bohun, an English knight with Edward's vanguard, mounted on a powerful horse, rode straight at Bruce with the object of killing him and ending the war at one stroke.

Bruce calmly awaited the attack. The Englishman was within a lance's thrust when he swung his horse to one side, and as the knight rode by brought his axe down upon his head, killing him instantly.

At dawn next morning the Scottish army heard their Mass. An abbot, barefooted and bareheaded, walked along the Scottish line holding a crucifix.

The whole Scottish army knelt.

From a distance the young King Edward watched with interest, and then fatuously cried : " See ! they are kneeling to ask mercy."

" Quite true," said one of his knights, " but it is from God, not from you. Those men are going to win or die."

" Be it so," said Edward. And he ordered the charge.

The fight began. Like the French at Waterloo, the English made repeated and desperate attempts to break through the Scottish ranks.

Time after time, the highly polished English army was thrown back with great slaughter. The English became dispirited, and perceiving this, Bruce brought up his reserves.

Then a diversion occurred which was fatal for the English. Suddenly, upon a hill near by appeared a crowd of men which looked like another Scottish army coming to the assistance of Bruce.

Actually, it was merely the attendants of the Scottish army who had picked up such arms as were handy and fastened blankets and sheets upon tent-poles for banners.

Whether this was a ruse previously arranged by Bruce is not known, but it had the effect of startling the English, who believed that they were being taken on their flank.

They began to give way, and immediately the Scottish king ordered the charge. The English fled in all directions and were pursued until they were a disorderly mob.

They lost 30,000 men, including 27 barons, 200 knights, and 700 esquires.

Thousands of prisoners fell into the hands of the Scots. According to one historian, " The chariot waggons, and wheeled carriages, which were loaded with baggage and military stores, would, if drawn up in a line, have extended for twenty leagues."

The English king, Edward, just managed to get away unscathed, and at length had to find refuge in the castle of Dunbar, thence escaping in a fishing skiff to Bamborough Castle.

Thus ended the battle of Bannockburn, one of the most important events in the history of Scotland. It secured the freedom and independence of the country.

Bruce immediately proposed a peace. His prisoners he treated with unusual leniency.

A commission was appointed, but when the English refused to give up their claims to feudal superiority over Scotland nothing came of the negotiations.

The war was resumed, but victory was generally on the side of the Scots.

In 1327 Edward II was deposed and murdered, and his son, Edward III, a youth of fourteen, succeeded. The regency prepared again to attack Scotland, but before they could do so, the Scottish army crossed the border and convinced the English that any further attempt to conquer Scotland would be futile.

The treaty of March 17, 1327, followed, by which the English king renounced all claims on Scotland.

Bruce died on June 7, 1329, and was buried at Dunfermline beside his second wife.

VIII

Edward II—England's Weakest King

EDWARD II was fond of pitch and toss. It was called " cross and pile " in those days, and Edward lost a lot of money at the game.

In a manuscript which gives a list of the expenses of this young popinjay of a king, there are many entries of small sums paid to the usher of his chamber for losses incurred.

He had little money of his own—or, rather, he was not allowed to handle it—so he borrowed from his barber the money to settle his bets.

Another interesting entry was a sum paid to a certain James, of St Albans, who entertained the King by dancing in front of him upon a table, causing him " to laugh heartily."

Still another item, which also concerns entertainment, relates to money paid to Morris Ken of the Kitchen, who made the King laugh heartily while hunting at Windsor by frequently tumbling off his horse.

The chief indiscretion of Edward II, surnamed Carnarvon, was that which concerned his favourite Piers de Gaveston, and ultimately led to his deposition.

Edward II was twenty-three when he succeeded his father. He had every prospect of a successful reign, for the trade of the country was improving, the Church was a really beneficial influence, the barons were in their places, and Wales was satisfied that a prince had been born within its borders.

That Edward was deficient in judgment and morality was shown when, even before his father had been placed in his grave, he ordered the imprisonment of a bishop who had protested against his early extravagances while a prince.

His next move was to recall to England Gaveston, his page. Gaveston was the son of a Gascon knight who had rendered the late King good service, and the boy had been introduced at Court as a reward for the fidelity of his father.

The two boys had been brought up together and had taken part in many scrapes. Once the young Edward was induced by Gaveston to break into the parks of the late King's treasurer.

Many other like indiscretions occurred, and Gaveston was banished the country.

On Gaveston's return to England he was created Earl of Cornwall, a title which had been reserved for members of the Royal house. When Edward went to France to bring back as his bride the daughter of the French king, he passed over the rest of the nobles and appointed Gaveston regent.

Edward called Gaveston " brother," and gave him the town of Wallingford as an estate.

Gaveston gave the best men in the kingdom nicknames, took all he could out of the Royal treasury and sent it abroad, while all business of the country was conducted through him.

He had to be present on every occasion that the people showed the King respect, and actually shared the honours.

At last the barons and the Commons met and sentenced Gaveston to perpetual exile.

Gaveston went back to France, but on the king of that country ordering his arrest, he took refuge in Flanders.

Suddenly he returned to England and was secreted by the King. On being discovered, he went to Scotland, where they refused to allow him to remain.

At last, with the object of trying to regain his former power, he returned publicly to the Court and was received with pleasure by Edward.

Again the barons held a meeting. Gaveston was excommunicated by the Archbishop of Canterbury, and a serious attempt was made to capture the erstwhile page.

To disguise the fact that the barons were meeting armed, the Earl of Lancaster arranged a tournament at York. Gaveston was hiding in the castle of Bamborough, and immediately the King heard what was afoot he hurried with his favourite to Tinmouth (Tynemouth).

They were followed by the barons, and here a distressing scene took place between Edward and his Queen, who was about to become a mother. She pleaded with him to give Gaveston up, but he refused, and the two men escaped by taking ship to Scarborough.

At last, through pressure, the King was compelled to leave the Gascon to his fate, and return to York and promise all the reforms the nobles demanded.

In return an oath was taken by the Earl of Pembroke that no harm should come to Gaveston pending negotiations.

Pembroke started for Wallingford with Gaveston as prisoner. They rested at a village between Oxford and Warwick, and while the Earl was temporarily absent Gaveston was captured by the Earl of Warwick and carried into the town accompanied by the jeers of the townspeople.

Pembroke feared for his life. He pointed out that he made an oath to keep Gaveston safe, but the nobles replied that they were acting in concert with the people, and Gaveston must die.

Warwick announced to the Gascon the manner of his death, whereupon the young man fell upon his knees, crying out : " Generous earl ! Pity me ! "

" Take him away ! " ordered the Earl in disgust.

Gaveston was taken out and handed over to two Welshmen. One stabbed him, and the other cut off his head.

For a time the murder had a most depressing effect upon the populace, particularly the inhabitants of Warwickshire, who were afraid that the King would take a drastic revenge. When it dawned upon them that the barons had the upper hand, they celebrated the deliverance in an appropriate way.

The King was indignant, and threatened reprisals. He collected the whole of his military forces, garrisoned his castles, and summoned a parliament of the barons.

They came to London prepared to stand their ground, and instead of going immediately to the King to announce their arrival, they sent a messenger to inquire the reason for their being called.

The Earl of Gloucester was appointed a go-between, and after some negotiation, in which the 1000 knights and 1500 foot-soldiers no doubt made an impression, the King decided to grant all their demands if they would agree to remove the stigma of traitor from the name of his late favourite.

They refused, and after further parley went back to their homes. The dispute petered out, and matters quietened down.

The next incident in this reign, the Battle of Bannockburn, was another blow to the King's prestige.

Robert Bruce had already taken Edinburgh and was besieging Stirling before Edward aroused himself from his lethargy.

Having awakened to the fact, he called together his

barons, but they argued that Parliament must sit first.
The King declined to convene a parliament, and ordered
the barons north.

Edward and his forces were beaten and chased for
fifty miles ; he himself escaped by taking a ship to
Berwick.

Edward had not learned his lesson. He appointed
two other favourites, the Despensers. The elder became
Earl of Winchester and the younger the Earl of Gloucester.

They confiscated the possessions of bishops and barons
who were known to be against the King, but it was the
beginning of the end when they attempted to cut down the
luxuries of the Queen.

She made an alliance with the disaffected persons,
and went over to France to secure aid. Mortimer, the
chief malcontent among the barons, escaped from the
Tower and joined her there.

The Queen levied an army from Hainault and Germany, the cost of which she paid out of the dowry through
the marriage of her son with Philippa, the daughter of
the Duke of Hainault.

With the Duke and Mortimer as commanders she
landed with her army at Orwell, on the Suffolk coast.
She increased her forces as disaffection gradually spread,
and crossed the country to Gloucester, where she demanded
the surrender of the elder Despenser. He was executed.

Eventually the King was persuaded to resign his
crown in favour of his son Edward, and he was placed in
confinement. Then the Queen began to conspire his
death.

Two knights, Gorney and Maltravers, were instructed
to take him from the custody of the Earl of Leicester and
expose him in every possible way to disease.

He was thinly clad, and was made to go with his
head uncovered ; they prevented him from sleeping,

4

shaved his head and beard, and took him on to the marshes near the Severn.

They shut him up in a loathsome chamber of a castle, but he was able to get air by enlisting the aid of two carpenters, who cut a hole for ventilation.

Edward still lived, and it was decided to kill him. One night two men went into his dungeon as he was sleeping, held him down, half suffocated him with the bolsters, and thrust a hot iron into his body.

> She-wolf of France, with unrelenting fangs,
> That tear'st the bowels of thy mangled mate.

EDWARD THE BLACK PRINCE
From the effigy on his tomb

IX

THE BLACK PRINCE WINS HIS SPURS

" Is my son dead ? " asked Edward III, anxiously.

" God forbid, sir," replied the messenger. " But he is hard beset, and your aid would be right welcome."

" Return to those who sent you," said the King, firmly, " and tell them from me they must not send for me to-day as long as my son is alive. Let the boy earn his spurs."

THE battle of Crécy was in progress. The Black Prince with a third of the English Army, supported by the Earls of Warwick and Hereford, John Chandos, and Godfroi d'Harcourt, commanded the vanguard.

New tactics were being employed—tactics which the King himself had evolved. The English men-at-arms had dismounted from their horses, and were fighting on foot the more numerous mounted men of France, the bravest and most efficient that the Kings of France and Bohemia could produce.

The Earls of Northampton and Arundel, in command of the Second Army, moved up to the assistance of the sixteen-year-old Prince, and yet the enemy appeared so overwhelming.

Immediately they sent a messenger to the King Edward, waiting in the rearguard, ready to fall upon the French at the right moment.

He dismissed the messenger, as already recorded, and added, " I desire, if it be God's will, that the day be his, and that the honour of it remain to him and to those I have appointed to support him."

And so the apparently unequal battle went on. The English soldiers became more confident, their commanders more persistent in their attacks.

On a hill Edward watched the progress of the fight. Gradually the French fell back. The Genoese bowmen in the French ranks were tired with a long march, but they continued to shoot fiercely with their crossbows.

The English archers caused great slaughter. The tide of battle was moving in favour of the English.

The blind King of Bohemia sensed how matters were drifting, and called upon his officers to lead him forward that he might strike at least one blow against the army of the Black Prince.

To save him from wandering away, they tied his bridle rein to their own bridles, and the King went before. Wielding his sword, he struck right and left.

But when the battle was over they found him dead with his party. The man who had slain the afflicted King had plucked three feathers from his crest, an eagle's pinion, and this became the symbol of the Prince of Wales.

The French losses were appalling. The King of Bohemia was dead, the Duke of Lorraine, the Earl of Alençon, the Count of Flanders, and eight other counts, two archbishops, seven lesser nobles, twelve hundred knights, and about 30,000 men had been lost.

Philip, the French King, escaped at the last moment. But Calais and Poictiers were to come.

Calais was reduced, and the battle of Poictiers was fought and won by the Black Prince alone, with a similar disproportion of troops.

Among the prisoners after this conflict was the French King John, son of Philip of Valois.

There was the same want of skill and strategy as at Crecy. Philip had failed as a commander, and in an attempt to retrieve his blunders had fought a hand-to-hand fight with his men.

John at Poictiers did the same, and fought on foot, battle-axe in hand. But his neglect of duty as a general could not be counterbalanced by his foolhardy bravery.

" Sir, yield you ! " shouted an English knight who had fought himself to within a sword-thrust of the French King.

" To whom shall I yield me ? " asked the King. " Where is my cousin, the Prince of Wales ? If I might see him I would speak to him."

" Sir, he is not here," was the reply. " I am Denis of Morbecque, a knight of Artois ; but I serve the King of England, because I am banished the realm of France, and I have forfeited all I had there."

Then the King, handing him his right gauntlet, said : " I yield me to you."

That night there was a celebration supper, and John was present. The courtesy of the Black Prince to his conquered foe is one of the classical instances of chivalry in history.

John was brought to England, and though captive, was treated with consideration. The terms of a treaty were formulated, and John went to France to put them before his nobles. When they were rejected, John returned to England in accordance with an undertaking that he would do so.

But all the energy, money, and time that had been spent in fighting France were in vain. There had been a great outpouring of blood. Villages and towns had been laid waste. The beautiful French countryside had been pillaged to no purpose.

For at the close of the reign of Edward III the subjugation of France was no nearer achievement.

If the Black Prince had proved a wonderful leader in

battle, his attributes of government were less conspicuous.
The war over, he returned to a condition which amounted
to obscurity.

At last he was entrusted with the government of
Gascony. He married his cousin Joan, the " Fair Maid of
Kent." They had two sons, Edward, who died in
infancy, and Richard, called from the place of his birth
Richard of Bordeaux, who afterwards became Richard II.

In the year 1365 Pedro the Cruel, King of Castile,
was deposed by his subjects. His bastard brother,
Enrique, was chosen in his place.

Pedro sought the assistance of the Black Prince.

The war went on during 1367, and, as a result of the
successes of the Black Prince, Pedro was restored to his
throne.

One of the chief battles in that campaign was at
Najara, where both sides made a brave display in their
shining armour before the fighting.

Here an incident took place which illustrates the
Black Prince's courtesy.

Sir John Chandos " brought his banner rolled up
together to the Prince and said, ' Sir, behold here is my
banner ; I require you to display it abroad and give me
leave this day to raise it.' "

The Spanish King and the Black Prince took the
banner and spread it, and, handing it back to Sir John,
they said : " Behold here your banner ; God send you
joy and honour thereof."

Carrying the banner to his company, Chandos remarked to his men : " Sirs, behold here my banner and
yours ; keep it as your own."

After this campaign the Black Prince returned home
disillusioned, for Pedro showed anything but gratitude.

The Black Prince was now ill, and Charles V of
France was challenging his feudal sovereignty.

It is probable that the Prince had failed to make himself popular with his subjects. At all events, they rallied round the banner of Charles, town after town revolting with a rapidity that aroused the Prince's anger.

He got up from a sick-bed at Angoulême, and took the field in person. He recaptured Limoges, where he massacred in cold blood 3000 of its citizens, and destroyed the town.

He never commanded at another military action.

In January, 1371, he resigned his government to the Duke of Lancaster and returned to England.

The later period of his life was spent more as a citizen than an administrator. Coventry became his home.

Here the guilds, which had been established by Edward III, were becoming prosperous.

In the reign of Henry VI they had reached such power that they found it necessary to build a hall in proportion to their dignity.

Verses were put in the hall to commemorate the Black Prince. They recorded that

The prince died in 1376, in his forty-sixth year, and was buried in Canterbury Cathedral. His father died twelve months later.

X

WAT TYLER AND THE "BEAUTIFUL BOY KING"

LUXURY and the sycophantic worship of the people of London were the cause of the ultimate downfall of Richard II, the " Beautiful Boy King."

When the son of the Black Prince and the Fair Maid of Kent rode from the Tower to Westminster to be crowned, it was an impressive and costly procession which accompanied the eleven-year-old child.

Thus wrote an old historian :

> There are around him a devoted multitude of nobles, knights, and esquires that dazzle his eye with their costly adornments. The streets they pass through on their gorgeously-caparisoned coursers are hung with floating draperies ; the windows are full of gazers. The air resounds with rapturous shouts, " God bless the Royal boy ! Long live King Richard ! "
>
> In Cheapside golden angels bend to him from the towers of mimic castles, presenting crowns ; and at other places he is met by beautiful virgins of his own age and stature, robed in white, who blow leaves and flowers of gold in his face and, as he approaches nearer, they fill gold cups from the conduits flowing with wine, and hand to him.
>
> High and low delight to honour him for his father's sake.

Young Richard was bewildered by this amazing display of magnificence. But already there was a cloud on the horizon. It hovered over Kent and Essex, where John Ball, " The Mad Priest of Kent," was carrying on a crusade among the peasantry, and advising the villeins to rise in favour of a demand to become free labourers.

On the top of this smouldering discontent came the Poll Tax of 1380 to pay for a disastrous war. The wage-owners, it was alleged, were not paying their share towards the expenses of the country. In 1377 all adults were required to pay one groat (fourpence) ; three years later it was increased to three groats.

Commissioners were appointed to collect the tax, and it was a dispute with one of these commissioners at Fobbing in Essex that led to the Great Revolt of 1381.

From Essex the revolt spread to Kent, then East Anglia, Middlesex, and Hertfordshire, while outside these areas there were isolated risings.

The rebels marched on London. The Kent men arrived at Blackheath and the men of Essex at Mile End on June 12. Two days later the Hertfordshire rebels appeared, and with this host outside the city walls the citizens became alarmed. It is probable that the insurgents would have been kept outside the city but for treason inside.

The only man of courage was the Lord Mayor, Walworth, the first to suffer at the hands of the rebels, who destroyed his house on the south side of the river.

" Let us parley ! " cried London's citizens, and with this end in view young Richard, now about fifteen, was taken by boat to the Surrey shore. The mission failed through the inflammatory harangues of John Ball.

The following day a treacherous act let in the rebels. The Kent men entered through the Bridge Gate and the Essex men through Aldgate. A systematic sacking of important buildings followed, with Wat Tyler, the Kent leader, directing operations. The Palace of the Savoy, the Temple, the Priory of St John of Jerusalem, and many others were partially burnt. Many foreigners were killed. The Government withdrew to the Tower, and with London in a state of panic, further offers were made for negotiation.

At Mile End, Wat Tyler and the boy King faced each other. Wat Tyler demanded the abolition of serfdom ; the villeins to remain in their holdings as free men, paying fourpence an acre for rent ; and the establishment of freedom to buy and sell wherever they chose. Furthermore, there was to be a free pardon for all the rebels.

Richard agreed to almost all the demands. Many insurgents started to return home, but Wat Tyler and others were dissatisfied. A further meeting between King and rebels was fixed for Smithfield next day, but was never held. Flushed with success, the rebel leader now demanded the abolition of all ecclesiastics except the friars.

A remark by one of the King's courtiers caused Tyler to bristle into a threatening attitude, whereupon Lord Mayor Walworth, producing a dagger, buried it to the hilt in Tyler's breast.

Then the fifteen-year-old King walked boldly up to the insurgents and engaged them in parley while Walworth roused the citizens. Without a leader the rebels were helpless. They dispersed. A day or two later the risings in the rest of the country collapsed.

Although this courage on the part of the King was a good augury for a wise reign, he soon began to show himself to be a weakling.

In 1382 he married Anne of Bohemia, on whom he lavished all his affection. When she died in 1394 he lost his mental balance. He would throw his clothes out of the window, and fits of temper left him so weak that it was a long time before he regained his senses.

Towards the end of the fourteenth century two parties evolved in the country. At the head of one was John of Gaunt, Duke of Lancaster, the other being under the

King's uncle, Thomas of Woodstock, Earl of Buckingham, who had been promoted to the Dukedom of Gloucester.

Suddenly Richard decided to assume full responsibility for the government of the country, but he was never able to control himself. He did, however, institute a third political party with himself at the head This led to intrigue and counter-intrigue, until the Duke of Lancaster was got rid of by appointing him a messenger to Spain on a fictitious mission.

When the Parliament of 1386 opened there were rumours that the King was seeking to murder all his opponents. To avoid trouble, Richard had to retire to Eltham, but Gloucester and Bishop Arundel, as spokesman for Parliament, followed him and demanded the dismissal of his ministers.

The King replied in anger that he would not dismiss a scullion at their behest. It was pointed out that not long before a king had been deposed, and Richard was asked to relinquish the control of expenditure.

The King gave way, and returning to Westminster, dismissed the chancellor and treasurer, a council being appointed to control the finances of the country, and more particularly the extravagances of the King's favourites and servants.

Richard soon began to conspire for the overthrow of the council. While the King was vainly trying to rouse the citizens of London, Robert Vere, Earl of Oxford, tried to raise a force in Chester, but, meeting the enemy at Radcot Bridge, refused to fight, and took flight to France. Thus the dominance of the court came to an end.

For a time things were quiet. The King secured peace with France which resulted in a thirty years' truce, the agreement being confirmed by the marriage of Richard to Isabella, the eight-year-old daughter of

Charles VI. This alliance caused some criticism in Parliament, but did not materially affect the apparent good relations between the King and Parliament.

Suddenly there came the King's crowning folly. Gloucester and his chief supporters were arrested, apparently in revenge for the events of a few years before. Henry of Bolingbroke, afterwards King Henry IV, and the Earl of Nottingham supported the King. Gloucester died in prison at Calais, Arundel was beheaded, and his brother Thomas, Archbishop of Canterbury, was exiled.

Richard now had complete control—but not for long, for the imposition of taxes to keep up his magnificent court soon set many friends against him, chief of whom was Henry of Bolingbroke. When Richard returned from Ireland in 1399, he was compelled to surrender to Henry, who had become a usurper of the crown.

In September he signed a deed of abdication on condition that his life was spared. He was sent secretly to Pontefract, where he died a year later. Shakespeare alleges that he was murdered. Richard was buried in state at King's Langley, and reinterred by Henry V in Westminster Abbey in 1413.

XI

Henry the Navigator—who never sailed

A GALE blew down the coast from the Bay of Biscay and rocked the castle of King John of Portugal at Oporto.

A frail, white-haired women raised her aching head from the pillow, and glancing round at her husband and her three sons, murmured : " What wind blows so strong against the house ? "

" The north wind," replied her husband.

" Then it is the wind for your voyage," the woman said.

And then, with another effort that taxed her waning strength, Philippa, the daughter of the English John of Gaunt, pleaded that her illness should not deter them from their contemplated crusade against the Moors.

" The Lord hath need of thy help," she whispered.

Prince Henry, the third son, gazed sorrowfully at his mother, and kneeling by the bedside placed his hand in hers.

It was his mother's inspiring words that assisted Henry in his subsequent campaigns and made him one of the most important figures in history—the man who laid the foundations and built the walls of Portugal's great colonial empire.

He was the founder of the Aviz dynasty, under which Portugal reduced Castile and conquered the Moors of Morocco, giving the country an important voice in the councils of Europe.

While his cousin, the English Henry V, was leading his starved and ragged army to victory at Agincourt, Henry of Portugal was gaining his laurels in Morocco. Landing at Ceuta, the "African Gibraltar," he led his men with conspicuous gallantry against the black hordes.

This battle of the Cross and the Crescent is described by old chroniclers, who give a vivid picture of the struggle with the Moslems making a stand at the very walls of the city, where the Christians were held up by a negro giant "who fought naked, but with the strength of many men, hurling the Christians to the earth with stones."

Then the negro was brought down by a lance thrust, and Ceuta fell.

Having established himself at Ceuta, Henry resolved to probe the secrets of Morocco by sending ships down the west coast of Africa, across the unknown ocean where men had never sailed before.

He thus began his explorations, which earned him the surname of "Navigator," although he himself never sailed on the expeditions.

In the year 1415, the year of Ceuta, he commissioned a certain John de Trasto for the expedition to find a passage to India, and thus bring Western Europe into direct contact with the treasures of the East, and to spread the Christian faith.

Henry established himself at Sagres (Cape St Vincent) and built a palace, a chapel, a study, an observatory (the earliest in Portugal), and a village for his men.

From these headquarters he sent sometimes single ships, sometimes huge armadas, to sail southward beyond the Cape of Nun, the utmost limit of navigation, beyond which, according to mariners, there was no return.

PRINCE HENRY THE NAVIGATOR

From an engraving

62

John de Trasto pushed the Portuguese influence to Grand Canary. This was not a voyage of discovery, for the Canarian Archipelago was well known to the French and Spaniards. It was not until ten years later that Henry really made a significant move towards a colonial empire for Portugal.

In 1424 he attempted to purchase the Canaries and began colonization. Three years later, in collaboration with his father, King John, he sent out an expedition to the Azores, and was gathering information about the coast of Guinea and the interior of Africa.

In 1433 the old king died, pleading with his son not to give up those schemes which, because of previous failures, such as the attempt to round Cape Bojador, were ridiculed for their costliness.

The following year one of the Prince's ships doubled the cape, and by the close of 1436 the Portuguese had almost reached Cape Blanco. In 1441 colonization was begun in earnest, and the first slaves and the first gold dust were brought back from the Guinea coasts.

In the meantime these successes were attracting the attention of merchants and seamen from Lisbon and Lagos, and hosts of adventurers offered themselves for the expeditions.

In 1443 the Prince was created a Knight of the Garter by Henry IV.

For forty years captains and crews of many nations sailed under licence from Henry. Year after year they pushed south, until they had explored 1350 miles beyond the charted world, and the North Star " was so low that it did almost seem to touch the sea."

Many strange tales were brought back to Henry the Navigator—tales of elephants and crocodiles, of natives with darts and spears tipped with poison. Some of the natives thought that the white men had been painted, and often tried to rub off the paint.

Stories were told of trees whose trunks were 108 spans round at the foot, and of the discovery of the four great rivers that flowed from the Garden of Eden.

One of the most interesting stories is that which concerns the discovery of the gold country, and how the leader of the expedition, Diego Gomez, made friends with a native king, who " always fastened his horse to a nugget of gold that twenty men could hardly move."

" We met," Gomez adds, " in a great wood, and he brought with him a vast throng of people with poisoned arrows, assegais, swords, and shields."

A formidable personage was this king, whose fierceness could be tempered only with the judicious use of port wine and biscuits.

The port wine, it appears, made him feel a new man, for, according to Gomez, who told the story to Henry, the King became " pleased and extremely gracious, giving me three negroes and swearing to me by the one and only God that he would never again make war against Christians, but that they might trade and travel through all the country."

All the information obtained by his navigators was sifted and studied by Henry, and gradually led to the first real map of the Old World.

Before this time maps had been either theoretical or the mere " scratchings of savages," having little regard to facts, and much to legend.

But the chart of Fra Mauro, which is a scientific review of Henry's explorations, crammed with detail and done on a vast scale, is the forerunner of the modern map.

Henry attended to the education and conversion to

Christianity of the hundreds of black slaves whom his captains brought back to Portugal, and founded colonies along the routes of exploration. He improved the art of shipbuilding, and did a great deal for navigation in regard to the perfection of instruments.

Henry was one of the greatest navigators the world has ever known, but, as we have said, he never went to sea himself. Seated in his study at Sagres, he directed his captains through the unknown seas in search of islands which, either through intuition or deduction, he thought existed.

He was stern but always generous, spending his days and often his nights at work, and following a rule of monkish asceticism.

Henry was born on March 4, 1394. He died on November 13, 1460, in his town near Cape St Vincent, and was buried in the church of St Mary at Lagos. A year later his body was removed to a monastery at Batalha.

His great-nephew, King Dom Manuel, had a statue of him erected at the church of Belem. In 1840 a monument was built to his memory at Sagres by the Marquis de Sà da Bandeira, while another statue has been placed in the Plaza Infante Henriquez at Oporto, close to the site of the palace where he was born.

The site of the palace is now partly occupied by a street officially named after him, but better known as the Rua dos Ingleses, so called because the English wine-merchants who owned the port-wine industry met there for centuries to transact their business.

It is not only the personal deeds of Prince Henry which will linger long in history, for the subsequent results of his labours have brought great advantages to the human race.

Only a comparatively small part of his task was

5

accomplished by himself. For forty years after his death his successors worked for the opening out of the African, or South-east, route to the Indies, and the Prince's share has been forgotten in the glory obtained by Diego Cam, Bartholomew Diaz, or Vasco da Gama.

XII

Joan, Fair Maid of Orleans

FIVE centuries have passed since that dramatic scene in the cobbled market-place of Rouen, and historians are still in doubt as to the responsibility for the burning of Joan of Arc, the Maid of Orleans.

The English, who were in occupation of the city, sanctioned the murder by adopting, like Pilate, an attitude of indifference.

They would, no doubt, have been satisfied with placing the girl under restraint but for the persistence of the ecclesiastics on both sides.

Even the French of Joan's own party made no attempt to rescue her. The cry of "Witch!" raised by the Church was sufficiently awe-inspiring for them to forget her military genius, which had been responsible for checking the English authority in France.

Joan, a French peasant's daughter, was born at the little hamlet of Domrémy, near the Meuse, on the borders of Champagne. The year of her birth is uncertain, but it was either 1410 or 1411.

Early in the fifteenth century a curious spirit prevailed in France. Town fought town for no apparent reason, and even remote villages rose against each other.

Joan, at the age of thirteen, was a wonder in her village at a time when the country places were riddled with superstition.

She herself became steeped with supernatural beliefs,

and sincerely believed in the prophecy that France would one day be saved by a virgin.

Constantly dreaming of this, it was not long before she thought she saw visions and heard voices. Once a great light seemed to appear, and from it came a voice which bade her be of good courage, for Heaven was protecting her.

This was taken by the girl as an approval of her dreams, and she set about preparing for the great work which she believed she was destined to fulfil.

Soon inspiration came frequently through the medium of her supernatural visitants.

At last she left her parents, intending to take up arms and drive the invader out of France, so that the young French King might be proclaimed at Rheims, the city of the coronation of French monarchs.

It was no small thing for a girl of thirteen to leave her home. If she faltered at the outset, there is little blame to her.

She had barely returned home when her native village was invaded by a party of Burgundians, who desolated the hamlet and destroyed its church.

It was at this time that the voices apparently became more insistent, pressing her to begin her mission.

She found herself told to go to de Baudricourt, the Governor of Vaucouleurs, and ask to be allowed to join the army.

She told him the story of the voices, but was laughed at and treated with contempt.

If the Governor disbelieved her, there were many who accepted her story. Among the converts to her faith were John of Metz and Bertram of Poulegny, who prevailed upon the Governor to allow them to take her to the Dauphin.

The Governor's permission was actuated by the

JOAN BEFORE THE ALTAR
Charles Buchel   68

desperate position of the French in Orleans, a city that was in a state of siege. Any hope was better than none.

When Joan appeared at court, her apparent supernatural powers were put to severe tests. She was called upon to recognize the French King Charles as he stood among his followers, there being no distinguishing mark or dress by which she could identify him.

She did it without hesitation.

But was her mission from Heaven or from the Devil?

The King and his courtiers were not satisfied. A council of ecclesiastics sat to decide the question. She refused to perform miracles and they showed doubt.

" Bring me to Orleans," she demanded, " and you shall see. The siege shall be raised, and the Dauphin crowned King of France ! "

It was impossible to damp her enthusiasm. They gave her a military command, and she dressed herself in armour.

In the church of Fierbois, she declared, they would find a sword buried near the altar.

A party of soldiers was sent, and digging at the spot indicated found the sword. This was accounted further evidence of her supernatural powers, but, in point of fact, Joan had lived at Fierbois for some time previously.

Soon afterwards, Joan, at the head of a body of French troops, entered Orleans. Thus encouraged, the French agreed to follow the girl—" La Pucelle " as she was called—in an attack on the English strongholds.

One after another they fell. The French army, believing that they had all the powers of Heaven on their side, fought with a ferocity that awed the English.

In one of the most desperate encounters, Joan was pierced by an arrow as she was about to mount a scaling ladder.

Taken away from the immediate scene of the battle,

she fainted.   When she regained consciousness and found
that her standard was in danger of capture, she forgot
her injury and once more led her men to the attack.

In a week Orleans was entirely freed from the English.
Then followed defeat after defeat for the invader, until
at the battle of Patey, John Talbot, Earl of Shrewsbury,
was beaten and taken prisoner.

Within three months Rheims opened its gates to the
Dauphin, and he was crowned King of France, exactly
in accord with the prophecy of the Maid of Orleans.

That having been achieved, the work of Joan of Arc
was finished.   The national spirit of France had been
awakened, and danger of ultimate defeat had now been
removed.

Then came the capture of Joan by the Burgundians,
who handed her over to the English.

The sequel was a trial which lasted for months.
Every attempt was made to drag from her the admission
that she was a sorceress.

The clever inquisitors were successful in the end.
They obtained from her a statement regarding her
visions.

What was more damning, she declared that she
would not submit to the ordinances of the Church, if the
voices advised her otherwise.

The issue of the trial was never in doubt.   She was
declared guilty of schism and heresy, and asked to recant.

When she refused, the scaffold was prepared at
Rouen.   The girl was brought forth, and the Bishop of
Beauvais read the indictment and sentence.

The pious prelates, partly English and partly French,
lifted their eyes in horror and deplored that such a young
and attractive girl should destroy both her body and
soul in such a wanton manner.

They could not be blamed ; it was the obstinacy of

the girl that was at fault, for the Church was inexorably opposed to witchcraft.

The stake and the faggots alarmed the miserable Joan. She muttered a word or two which her tormentors took for an expression of contrition.

They immediately produced a written confession and induced her to make a mark on the document, as she was unable to write her name.

She was taken back to prison under a sentence of perpetual imprisonment.

But her French enemies were conspiring to obtain her death. Though the ecclesiastical council was prepared to accept any sign which might conceivably be taken as a retraction the Burgundians were determined.

Her male attire was placed in her prison cell in the hope that she might put it on and thus show that her confession had been false.

She did put it on, and as she clothed herself the voice began to speak and reproach her for her lack of courage.

When the gaoler came to her cell she was wearing her uniform, and, being led out again, she told her persecutors :

" What I resolved I resolved against truth ; let me suffer my sentence at once, rather than endure what I suffer in prison."

The scaffold was set up, the faggots prepared, and before a great sea of pale upturned faces, with the ecclesiastics, French and English, looking on, she was taken in tears to the stake.

The sun, which had been obscured by the pinnacle of the cathedral, suddenly illuminated the shadowy market-place, and the smoke of the burning faggots drifted aimlessly into the narrow thoroughfares which led away from the square.

The bishops on their elevated gallery gazed down

upon the scene, tight-lipped in their endeavour to show no emotion.

As the flames rose higher one of them, with tears in his eyes, left his seat, saying, " I can stand no more ! "

He was Cardinal Beaufort, the Englishman.

XIII

MICHELANGELO, IMPECUNIOUS SCULPTOR

WHEN Michelangelo with great pride started to work on his famous mausoleum of Pope Julius II, he little knew what was in store for him.

The Pope had a curious temper, and as the sculptor had a far from prepossessing appearance and a somewhat modest demeanour, Julius used to treat him at times with contempt.

Michelangelo had worked about two years upon his masterpiece when funds ran out. He had spent his small fortune on the project.

The Cathedral of St Peter was too small for the magnificent creation, so Julius decided to build a new one, and entrusted the task to Bramante, his favourite architect, who was not friendly to Michelangelo.

There came a day when the workmen of Michelangelo refused to go on without pay.

"Wait," he said. "I will go to the Pope for the last time, and if he does not pay me I will pay you if I have to mortgage my soul and body to the Devil."

He was then a few years over thirty, a small man, bony but thick-set, with a huge head, scanty hair, and a coarse black beard. He had a broken nose, the result of a fight as a boy.

The Pope had just finished dinner when Michelangelo was shown in. At the feet of the Pontiff was a boy playing a lute.

73

The Pope glanced at Michelangelo with a bored expression, which was not encouraging to the sculptor.

Then Julius ran his eyes over the accounts and drawings which Michelangelo produced, and said imperiously, " I haven't time. Come on Monday."

" But the workmen are asking to be paid," said the sculptor. " If your treasurer does not pay the money, I must buy the marble for your mausoleum out of my own pocket."

Julius did not reply. With a sweep of his arm he threw the documents to the floor, and, giving no further attention to Michelangelo, he arose from his chair and walked to the inner chamber for his midday rest.

The sculptor borrowed money and paid his men.

On the following Monday he presented himself again at the Palace, but this time was not allowed to enter.

He returned home and wrote a note to the Pope telling him that if he wanted Michelangelo he must look for him elsewhere than in Rome.

He then set out for Florence, his native place, and, having arrived at the old fortress of Pogibonci, the first town in Florentine territory, he put up for the night.

Here messengers from the Pope arrived and threatened to take him back by force, but he reminded them that he was now on Florentine territory, and the Pope had no jurisdiction.

He wrote a letter to the Pope telling him he would not return at any price, and the messengers took it to Julius.

A few months afterwards Julius issued a Papal Bull to the noblemen of Florence, stating that he wished Michelangelo to return, and if he did so he would be forgiven.

The sculptor ignored this Bull and also the second, which followed quickly, and began to treat with an emissary of the Sultan who had been anxious to get his services for years.

Then came the third Bull, making Michelangelo a Florentine ambassador, thus giving him immunity from molestation, together with the Pope's assurance that he was " loved and appreciated."

To these blandishments the sculptor fell, and met the Pope at Bologna, where, to his disgust, he was ordered to make a huge statue of Julius. This took him sixteen months.

At the end of this work he returned to Rome, hoping that the Pope would allow him to continue with the mausoleum.

But Julius had other views. Bramante, the architect, was anxious to cause another quarrel between the Pope and his sculptor, and, at the same time, secure favour for his protégé, Raphael. He had induced the Pope to order the painting of the roof of the Sistine Chapel.

Hoping that Michelangelo would refuse the job, as he had declared he would do no more painting, he was annoyed when Michelangelo agreed to carry out the task.

Bramante was commissioned to put up the scaffolding, but made such a mess of it that Michelangelo had to take it down and rebuild it.

After dismissing his painter-assistants because of their inefficiency, he worked for months at the painting, lying flat on the platform many feet above the floor of the chapel.

His body became so used to this painful position that he was unable to stand up without reeling. He was losing his sight, and suffered from sleeplessness and giddiness. He could only read by holding a paper above his head and looking upwards.

For weeks at a time he never left the scaffolding, and

he and his labourer lived, slept, and ate just beneath the roof of the scaffold.

When he did occasionally come down, he wandered about the streets of Rome like a lost child.

One day the Pope came and insisted upon looking at Michelangelo's work, much to the painter's disgust, for he knew that Julius was about to complain.

He argued that the painter was taking too long over the work and that it was unnecessary for him to put in all the details, such as veins and muscles in the figures.

" I want you to finish it before I die," the Pope said peevishly. " When do you expect to finish the ceiling if you paint every vein and muscle ? "

" I cannot work any differently," the painter replied, and then told the Pope he had better get some one to finish the work.

There followed a quarrel, and the Pope, shaking with anger, struck the artist twice with his stick.

The same evening the Pope apologized and was ready to make peace with Michelangelo at any price.

In 1512 the scaffolding was pulled down, and the ceiling stood revealed. It depicted the creation of the earth and the sky, of the sun and moon, the waters and plants, and of the first man, Eve, the fall, the sacrifice of Cain and Abel, the flood, and Noah, Shem, and Ham.

Underneath there were a number of prophets, sybils, and giants ; lower down were pictures of life at Nazareth.

After examining the ceiling critically, Julius embraced the painter. " Glory be to you, Buonarroti," he said ; " glory be to me as well, for had I not persisted and pestered you, you would never have finished."

Thirty years after, Buonarroti wrote that all the disagreements between him and Julius had been due to his enemies, who had conspired for his overthrow, including Bramante and Raphael, who, he declared, had learned all his art from him.

Michelangelo was the son of the Governor of Caprese. His foster-mother was a stonemason's wife, and as the child grew up among the stone-carvers he soon become used to the mallet and chisel.

At the age of thirteen he was apprenticed to a painter, Ghirlandaio, who complained, " This boy knows more than I do."

His work attracted the attention of Lorenzo " the Magnificent," and he was taken into the palace, where he fell in love with Luigia de Medici. It was about this time, too, that he was struck by one of his fellow-students, who broke his nose.

He left for Venice, but, being unable to get work, went to Bologna, but soon had to leave because of the jealousy of other craftsmen in the town.

In 1495 he returned to Florence, and then was called to Rome by a cardinal who had bought a piece of his work. At the age of twenty-six he went back to Florence, known as the greatest sculptor of his age. It was in this city that he made his great masterpiece, the colossal David.

Pope Julius died with the mausoleum uncompleted. The new Pope Leo X ordered Michelangelo to Florence to erect a tomb in honour of his two brothers who had just died.

At the age of fifty-two he was back in Rome at the bidding of Pope Paul III, and when over sixty fell in love with Vittoria Colonna, the widow of the Marquis of Pescara, but he saw her die in a nunnery.

Having always kept his relatives, Michelangelo died poor on February 18, 1564, after a chill.

He had claimed to be a sculptor rather than a painter, and that is no doubt why he signed his paintings in the Sistine Chapel as Michelangelo instead of his surname.

Nine years before his death the huge Julian tomb was completed, but Michelangelo had to employ modified designs.

He was rugged, stern, and uncompromising—the antithesis of Raphael, who had such courtier-like ways and so many assistants working under his direction.

The only sculpture that Michelangelo signed was "La Pieta," a marble group representing the Madonna tending the body of the dead Christ, which was executed in 1499.

XIV

QUEEN ELIZABETH, A CINDERELLA OF HISTORY

THE experiences of Queen Elizabeth were unlike
those of many of the earlier English sovereigns
in the fact that her troubles came before instead of after
her coronation. As a young girl she was continually
threatened with death, owing to the machinations of one
or other of those who were aspiring to the Crown.

She was not wanted by her father, Henry VIII, after
he had disposed of her mother, Anne Boleyn, and from
time to time she was put away with one guardian and then
another, the child herself failing to understand what it
all meant until she was about ten years old, but all the
time trying to ingratiate herself with her more fortunate
relatives.

At the outset she disgraced herself by being a daughter
instead of a son.

The birth was described by the Spanish Ambassador
as " of great disappointment to the King, and a shame
and confusion to the astrologers, wizards, and witches,
all of whom had foretold the arrival of a lusty son."

Elizabeth had barely cut her teeth when couriers
were sent out to find her a husband. The first on the list
of prospective bridegrooms was the Duke of Angoulême,
third son of Francis I of France. It was suggested that
the young Duke should be sent to England to be educated
as an English gentleman.

This did not meet with the approval of the French.

It was not long after these attempts to arrange a

79

suitable marriage that Elizabeth was cast aside. The shadow of the scaffold was looming around her mother, Anne Boleyn. Henry was paying attentions to Jane Seymour in the hope in getting an heir. The young princess was removed from the sight of the court and handed over to Lady Bryan for upbringing and education.

Anne was executed, and Jane Seymour gave birth to the long-awaited heir to the throne, Prince Edward. Elizabeth became the Florence Dombey of the King's household.

As stepmother after stepmother passed in review, Elizabeth tried to keep on good terms with all of them. She wrote frequently to Jane Seymour and Anne of Cleves precocious letters which amazed every one. At the age of thirteen her Italian master declared : " She has a singular wit and marvellously meek stomach."

Katharine Parr appeared on the scene, and she it was who influenced the King to allow Elizabeth to return to the court.

Henry's death made life more bearable for Elizabeth. Young Edward became the Sixth, and the succession thereafter was vested firstly in Mary, the daughter of Katharine of Aragon, and then in Elizabeth. But the clouds were gathering again, for Katharine Parr, who had been a kind of fairy godmother to the young princess, died.

Sir Thomas Seymour was arrested for trying to scheme a marriage with Elizabeth with the object of gaining the throne on the possible death of Edward, who was a weakling. Elizabeth was charged with being an accessory, and a statement which was described as a confession was wrung from her. For a time she adopted a meek attitude, and then suddenly demanded that the false tales and scandal about her should be denied officially.

QUEEN ELIZABETH

A contemporary engraving by Crispin van der Passe after a drawing by Isaac Oliver

Seymour was executed, and matters settled down quietly, Elizabeth writing affectionate letters to her half-brother, the King.

Then came the death of Edward, and the attempt by the Duke of Northumberland to place Lady Jane Grey on the throne. The insurrection over, Mary and Elizabeth were driven through the streets of London for the coronation of the former. To the annoyance of Mary, Elizabeth received the greater ovation.

Not long afterwards Elizabeth became an innocent victim of the rising of Sir Thomas Wyatt. She was brought to the Court by force, despite her indisposition, and on the way to the palace was greeted with cheers by the populace.

Mary had ordered her sister to London, but was apparently in no mind to give her an audience. At last the Queen's counsellors suggested to Elizabeth that she should throw herself at the feet of Mary and beg for pardon. She declared she had done nothing to merit this treatment. She wrote to Mary asking for an interview, but this had no effect, and next day she was taken down the river and into the Traitors' Gate of the Tower.

She was confined in the fortress for a month under rigid discipline. If she wished to open her casement window she had to obtain an order from the Council. In the meantime she was subjected continually to a close examination as to her complicity in the Wyatt rebellion.

At last, according to an historian :

> On Saturdaye, at one of the cloke at afternoone the Lady Elizabeth was delyv'd out of the Tower and went to Richmond on her way to Woodstock.

Woodstock proved to be another prison. Sir Henry Bedingfield, her guardian, was ordered to keep the princess under the strictest supervision. If she asked

6

for books he was almost afraid to give them to her, and when she asked for a Bible it was accounted as heresy.

Months passed, and at last Elizabeth was requested to go to Hampton Court Palace. Here she was interrogated again, but still protested her innocence of any conspiracy. At the instance of Philip of Spain, Mary's husband, the Queen consented to see the Princess, and for a time Elizabeth remained at Court. Later she went to live at Hatfield.

In the meantime attempts were being made to marry her to an eligible prince. The ten-year-old son of Philip of Spain was suggested, but Elizabeth successfully resisted these efforts. She was now twenty-three, " slender and straight, well favoured, but high nosed, of limbs and features neat."

One morning in November, 1558, the long-expected news was brought to the House of Commons that Mary was dead. After shedding crocodile tears at the end of the woman who had bathed the country in blood, the members shouted : " God save Queen Elizabeth ! "

The coronation was held with great rejoicing and the expenditure of a great deal of money.

Immediately Elizabeth's counsellors began to look around for a suitable husband. The country, too, was insistent that she should marry as soon as possible.

A deputation headed by the Speaker of the House of Commons called upon her urging that she should marry " and bring forth children, heirs of both of your Majesty's virtue and empire, thus continuing immortal."

She dismissed the deputation with an excuse, and as a result the country was flooded with pamphlets advocating the Queen's marriage.

But Elizabeth was not a marrying woman, and when she fell ill, Mary Queen of Scots was freely mentioned as a successor. The years passed and Elizabeth remained a spinster.

The first ten years of her reign were tranquil, as were also her last years.

Her character was adequately summed up by Castelnau, the French Ambassador :

> She has prospered in all her affairs, and continues to do so. Not from possessing great wealth, or from granting large donations, for she has always been a great economist, but without exacting from her subjects in the manner of her predecessors. Her great desire has been the repose of her people. Hence the nation has become exceedingly rich during her reign. But however unusual her ability, she has never undertaken great affairs on her own judgment, but has always conferred with her council. Careful to keep out of wars, she has thrown them upon her neighbours rather than drawn them upon herself.
>
> She has been taxed with avarice, but unjustly, and because she has refused to be free in her gifts. She discharged all the debts of her predecessors, put her own finances into good order, and amassed great riches without imposing any new tax upon her people.

XV

Mary Queen of Scots—Her Loves and Hates

AFTER Mary Queen of Scots had nursed the Earl of Darnley through an attack of measles, she determined to marry him.

Mary's second matrimonial venture was no better than her first, when she married the Dauphin of France.

Darnley was not a saint, and Mary soon found that he was more attracted by the roseate hues of kingship than by her own blandishments.

Moreover, his affections were liable to be diverted very easily—as easily as hers.

There was soon trouble between them, but fear of the same enemies kept them together for a time for reasons of mutual preservation.

The two young people were cousins. He was the son of Matthew Stuart, Earl of Lennox, a master of intrigue, who had been exiled in France for twenty years, and who had apparently passed on to his son his capacity for political juggling, and other things far more reprehensible.

Queen Elizabeth, characteristically meddlesome, tried to stop the marriage by producing a husband for Mary who would support her own claim to the Scotch throne.

Lord Robert Dudley, her choice, had already made himself a reputation that caused a good deal of twittering in court dovecots. He was suspected of murdering his wife, Amy Robsart.

The young lovers, in their early twenties, turned their backs on Elizabeth, and got married in secret in Stirling Castle, the appropriate Catholic rites being celebrated in the apartment of David Rizzio, the Queen's French secretary, who in the end was the first of the trio to meet a tragic death.

At the same time Mary assured the English ambassador—in response to a direct inquiry from Queen Elizabeth as to her intentions—that the marriage to Darnley would not take place for three months, a respite which satisfied Queen Elizabeth for a time.

But on July 29, 1565, they were remarried at Holyrood, and Elizabeth appeared resigned to the inevitable.

Eighteen months later Darnley was murdered.

The young couple started rather inauspiciously by incurring the hatred of two powerful enemies, the Earls of Morton and Glencairn.

Then, upon the stage of this drama, appeared James Hepburn, Earl of Bothwell, who later became Mary's third husband.

The atmosphere at Holyrood was becoming charged with explosive matter. The Earl of Murray and the Earl of Glencairn objected to the Catholic character of the marriage, and with a body of troops began an advance on Edinburgh, but were compelled to fall back on Dumfries before the advance of the royal army.

In its ranks was the Earl of Bothwell, who had just returned from a three years' forced exile in France.

In 1562 Bothwell had been accused of trying to seize the Queen with a view to handing her over to the Earl of Arran, a lunatic.

Pressed by her enemies, the Queen appealed to France for help, but the French Ambassador advised her to make peace with the revolutionaries. The Queen rejected the advice, and in October, 1565, with an army of 18,000 dispersed the malcontents, Murray being compelled to seek shelter in England.

Darnley, egged on by his father, began to aspire to the throne in his own right, and hereupon David Rizzio became a factor in the moving drama of Holyrood.

When Darnley sent his request to the Queen, Rizzio advised her to refuse this " hazardous and audacious " demand.

Darnley, ever an opportunist, joined forces with the enemies of Mary and her secretary. When the Queen was invited by the King of Spain to join his league for the suppression of Protestantism, and Rizzio was given the office of chancellor left vacant by Morton, the Protestant nobles became angry.

This already delicate situation was further complicated by another affair of the heart on the part of the Queen. Darnley was becoming convinced of his wife's infidelity, and, according to one account, put his suspicions to the test, with the result that he found the foreign secretary in the private apartment of the Queen at midnight.

He told his uncle, George Douglas, and Douglas seized the opportunity of setting Darnley against his wife by adding more fuel to the young man's anger.

He declared that Rizzio was now the Queen's lover, and Darnley, needing little persuasion to believe it, became a more ardent supporter of the enemies of the Queen.

A bond was signed in which Darnley pledged himself to support the revolutionaries, who, on their side, undertook to punish " certain privy persons " offensive to the State, " especially a stranger Italian called Davie."

In Newcastle, Murray and the other nobles awaited their chance, secure in the fact that Darnley had pledged himself to obtain their freedom and restoration to office.

On March 9 the Palace of Holyrood was surrounded by troops under the command of Morton, and Rizzio was taken by force from the presence of the Queen and murdered.

Darnley then discharged Parliament in the name of himself, as King, and next day the banished lords returned to Edinburgh.

They were guarded by two thousand horsemen under the command of Bothwell, who had escaped from Holyrood on the night of the murder of Rizzio with the object of raising an army on behalf of the Queen, but following Darnley's *coup* was content to obey orders.

By now the Queen was trembling for her crown, and had no option but to receive the banished nobles with as much grace as possible, with an undertaking to sign a bond for their security.

The temporary reconciliation with Darnley did not make the Queen any more popular. The " King " was scorned by all parties, and no one cared to be seen in his company.

The Queen soon wormed from him the story of the plot for the assassination of Rizzio. He gave the ringleaders completely away, and one by one Mary got rid of them by banishment.

On June 19, 1566, she gave birth to a son (afterwards James I of England), but this did not improve Darnley's position.

At first he refused to claim parentage, and at last was compelled to admit that he was the father.

Darnley, ostracized by everybody, prepared to escape to France, but in face of a resolve by the Queen to keep him in the country, had to remain.

He was asked, in the presence of the French Ambassador and an assembly of nobles, to speak out and declare what he had against the Queen.

Eventually he said he had nothing to allege.

By now Mary was showing much favour to Bothwell, who, with his newly-won power, became insolent and arrogant. Once, when he was dangerously wounded by a notorious outlaw, Mary rode twenty miles through the wild country to visit him.

Immediately on his recovery Bothwell laid a proposal before the Queen for her divorce from Darnley, supported by Murray, Huntly, Argyle, and Lethington, who undertook to dispose of the " King " without prejudice to the heir.

She agreed on the condition that the child's legitimacy was not called into question.

A few days afterwards the child was baptized. Darnley was not present.

One report states that he was not allowed to attend the christening festivities, while another asserts that he refused to attend on his own initiative.

After the ceremony Darnley was struck down by sickness that suggested poison. He was taken to his father at Glasgow, and when it was learned that he was recovering, a further determination was made to murder him.

On January 22, 1567, the Queen visited her husband and proposed that he should be removed to Craigmillar Castle, where he could have the benefit of medicinal baths.

Instead, he was taken to the lonely Kirk o' Field, the squalid house between the ruins of two sacred buildings in the neighbourhood of the notorious Thieves' Row.

On the evening of Sunday, February 9, the Queen took the final farewell of the miserable reprobate.

The scene was now set. In the dead of night a terrific explosion shook the city, and the building in which Darnley had been placed was blown to fragments.

Darnley and his servant apparently had a premonition of a tragedy, for they attempted to escape over a wall. Next day the two bodies were found in the grounds of an adjacent building—strangled, no doubt, by Bothwell's attendants.

Three months and six days after the murder of her husband, Mary married Darnley's murderer. The hypocrisy of Mary is laid bare at once by her writing to the Bishop of Glasgow and her Ambassador in France, announcing that she had escaped providentially from an attempt on her life as well as that of her husband.

A reward of two thousand pounds was offered for the apprehension of the murderer !

But Edinburgh was by no means in favour of this drastic way of removing Darnley, and Bothwell was openly denounced as the murderer.

At night in the streets voices could be heard crying out for vengeance against the conspirators, and the Queen's name was freely coupled with the demands.

Four days after the bodies were found Darnley was buried in the Chapel of Holyrood with secrecy equal to that observed at the funeral of Rizzio.

On the following Sunday Mary left Edinburgh and, it is said, passed her time in shooting-matches with Bothwell and others.

Darnley's father pleaded for justice and the punishment of the murderers, but the Queen did not move, and openly declared her purpose to marry Bothwell. On May 3 Bothwell's wife obtained a divorce, after an alliance which lasted a little over a year.

The subsequent marriage led to an insurrection, and Mary was confined in various prisons in Scotland and England until 1587, when she was accused of further conspiracy and executed.

XVI

Sir Francis Drake, Sea-Bandit

BESIDES the one about the game of bowls on Plymouth Hoe, many stories are told of Sir Francis
Drake.

Some of them are apocryphal. Here is a specimen :

> Drake was off on a long voyage and, having a presentiment
> that he might not return, he gave his wife permission to marry
> again after a certain period of years.
>
> Time passed. Drake tarried. His wife turned down several
> good offers, but at last she decided to go to the altar.
>
> Drake had gone West and was thousands of miles away.
> But, having second sight, he knew, so the story goes, what was
> going on.
>
> He took immediate precautions to stop the bigamy.

There are two versions of the sequel.

In the first Drake is said to have loaded a big gun
and fired the projectile through the earth.

It was a good shot.

The cannon ball fell between the bride and bridegroom just as Madam Drake was about to say " Yes."

" That," cried the bride, " comes from Drake !
While he lives there must be neither troth nor ring
between thee and me ! "

The second version, which was also believed in the
West Country for long afterwards, was that a stone fell
upon the bride's train as she was on the way to church.

She believed that it came from her husband, and
turned back.

SIR FRANCIS DRAKE

The stone, it is said, is still there. For though it has been taken away on many occasions it has found its way back in a mysterious manner.

They were much concerned in Elizabethan days that Drake might fall over the edge of the world. He had a habit of wandering too far a-sea. Soon or late he would reach that great gulf which divided the top side from the underside of the flat earth.

Sure enough he did.

And when he had safely crossed the gulf he turned to his men with a triumphant smile and asked if any one knew where he was.

Up spake a cabin boy.

" Sir," he said, " we are just under London Bridge."

Whereupon Drake immediately threw the lad overboard for knowing too much. " If I let thee live," he said, " there will be one man greater than myself."

The story of the game of bowls has a version which is even more miraculous than that of the cannon ball.

After Drake had finished his game, he sent for a hatchet and a block of wood. He chopped the wood into small pieces and cast them into the sea. Immediately they turned into a fleet of ships, and thus the Spanish Armada was vanquished.

Having achieved fame and a handle to his name, Drake decided that it was time he had a coat of arms.

There was another family named Drake, with a somewhat ornate coat of arms. He decided to use this.

The other Drakes objected. The head of that house, Bernard Drake, also a sea-captain, meeting Francis at Court, struck him.

There was uproar. The men were about to fall to with their swords when Elizabeth appeared, stopped the fight, and appeased Francis by offering him a new coat of arms much more distinguished than the one he had appropriated.

The absurd stories told of Drake indicate the awe of him in the popular mind.

Actually he was just a buccaneer, and no better than other pirates of his day.

That he generally confined himself to ravaging the property of Spain was due to the fact that he had an intense hatred of Spaniards, who had been responsible, in a treacherous way, for the ruin of his first enterprise.

Drake was born in a cottage on the banks of the river Tavy. The year of his birth is doubtful, but it is generally believed to have been in 1544.

Drake's family were poverty-stricken and the lad was apprenticed to the master of a small coasting barque. The owner of the ship died without an heir and left the vessel to Drake in return for his faithful service.

In the course of time Drake saved a fair sum of money and decided to join in an expedition to the New World then being organized by Captain John Hawkins.

While they were in the Bay of Mexico, the apparently friendly Spaniards attacked them and sunk four ships. Drake was ruined.

He applied to Spain for compensation, and petitioned Queen Elizabeth, but without success.

He vowed revenge on the Spaniards, and decided, so soon as he was able, to make them suffer for their treachery.

He made two preliminary voyages to America to discover information concerning the situation of the Spanish settlements in the West Indies, and then began to fit out an expedition by means of which he hoped to obtain his revenge and, at the same time, to make himself rich.

On July 21, 1572, with two small ships totalling 95

tons and 75 men and boys, he landed at Port Pheasant, the granary of the West.

A little distance inland he saw a wreath of smoke, and going forward to investigate, he found a fire in the top of a high tree. Nailed to another tree was a lead plate with the following warning engraved on it :

Captain Drake ! If you fortune to come to this port, make haste away ! For the Spaniards which you had with you here the last year have betrayed this place, and taken away all that you left here. I depart hence this present 7th of July, 1572. Your very loving friend, JOHN GARRETT.

Drake stayed at this port long enough to build his pinnaces. At the end of a week a barque in command of John Rowse of the Isle of Wight arrived, and being told of Drake's scheme, Rowse decided to join the adventurer.

The expedition went on to Nombre de Dios. They approached at dead of night, intending to attack the town at daybreak. But realizing the strength of the place, Drake decided to land by the light of the moon.

They reached the market-place before being opposed, but here they were greeted with shots. Drake retaliated with a flight of arrows which drove the Spaniards off. Entering the house of the governor, they found a huge quantity of silver which had been brought from the Panama mines.

They decided to leave the silver and raid the king's treasure-house instead. Here there were gold and jewels in abundance, if rumours were correct.

They found the place well defended. During the attack Drake received a wound in the leg, and the whole party were forced to retreat. Drake was carried to his pinnace, and sail was set for a small island about a league away.

After a period of convalescence, Drake decided to attack Panama. There they were more fortunate. They captured a mule train loaded with treasure, including several tons of silver. The silver was buried and afterwards recovered by the Spaniards, but the rest of the treasure was carried to the English ships.

Drake arrived at Plymouth on August 9, 1573.

It was a Sunday, and the church bells were ringing for service. The news of Drake's arrival soon spread over the town, and those sitting in the pews darted out to welcome their hero with the other crowds.

Four years later, Drake determined upon a voyage in the South Seas. Before he left, the Queen gave him a sword, saying : " Receive this sword, Francis Drake, and wear it until we require it of thee again. We do account that he that striketh at thee, Drake, striketh at us ! "

Drake was thus assured of official recognition by the sovereign. He set out blithely with five vessels of different sizes, well manned to the number of 164 men, "'gentlemen," and sailors. He had several pinnaces in frames ready to put together as he had in his previous expedition.

With him he carried " expert musicians, rich furniture, with divers shows of all sorts of curious workmanship, whereby the civility and magnificence of his native country might, among all nations whither he should come, be the more admired."

He concealed his destination, and, after many adventures, he reached the Straits of Magellan. He was the second European to attempt the passage of the Straits. On September 6, 1578, he entered the South Sea.

There he met Balboa, the Spaniard, who considered himself master of the South Seas.

Drake decided to dispute the Spaniard's possession,

but a gale drove the English ships away before they could get to close quarters.

However, they captured a Spanish ship well laden with treasure. The silver alone was valued at £212,000.

Drake then steered his ship, the *Golden Hind*, for home. After many perilous experiences they arrived at Plymouth, where he was again greeted with the utmost enthusiasm.

On going to the Court to make his report, he received a gracious reception from the Queen. She ordered Drake's ship to be drawn into a creek at Deptford, to be preserved as a monument of the most memorable voyage the English had yet undertaken.

She paid the ship a visit, and a great banquet was held on board.

After the feasting the Queen said : " Francis Drake, we entrusted a sword to thy keeping till we demanded it of thee again. We now require thee to deliver it up in the manner in which thou receivedst it from our hands."

Drake knelt and presented the scabbard. The Queen took it, and drawing out the sword, exclaimed : " 'Tis a sword that might serve thee yet, Drake, although thou has carried it round the world. But ere we return it to thee, it must render us a service."

Stepping back, she smote the adventurer on the back and cried, " Rise up, Sir Francis Drake ! "

There was a shout of applause from the spectators. But suddenly the bridge on which the crowd was standing collapsed, and a hundred people were thrown to the ground. Fortunately none suffered more than a sprain or a bruise.

Drake was given the post of Vice-Admiral in the fleet which dispersed the Armada.

Six years later he and Sir John Hawkins took a fleet

to the West Indies and destroyed the town of Nombre de
Dios.

Soon afterwards Drake fell ill, and was obliged to
keep his cabin. On the morning of January 28, 1596,
he rose and dressed himself. But his actions were those
apparently of a drunken man. He was seriously ill.

In an hour he died. His body was placed in a leaden
coffin, and lowered into the sea to the volley of musketry
and a salvo from all the guns of the fleet.

XVII

SIR WALTER RALEIGH, HERO OF HIS OWN
EXECUTION

> Even such is Time, that takes on trust
> Our youth, our joys, our all we have,
> And pays us but with earth and dust ;
> Who, in the dark and silent grave,
> When we have wander'd all our ways,
> Shuts up the story of our days ;
> But from this earth, this grave, this dust,
> My God shall raise me up, I trust.

THESE words were written by Sir Walter Raleigh on the fly-leaf of a Bible on the night before his execution.

In Old Palace Yard, Westminster, the scaffold was being built.

Dawn came, and with it thousands of London's citizens.

There were some who anticipated with satisfaction the end of Raleigh, the favourite of the dead Queen Elizabeth. More honest people declared that it was murder, actuated by the avarice of James I, the Scottish coxcomb who now held the dual crown.

There was an affecting parting between Raleigh and his wife. The tears coursed down her cheeks as she told him that the king had " graciously " given her permission to dispose of the body as she thought fit.

" It is well, Bess," he said with a smile, " that thou mayest dispose of that dead thou hadst not always the disposing of when alive."

7   97

The Dean of Westminster administered the sacrament. Raleigh professed his trust in God, and forgave all, especially those who had engineered his death.

He made light of his coming execution and remarked, " I would rather thus end my days than by a burning fever. I thank God who hath imparted to me strength of mind never to fear death."

The doomed man was led out, and on the way to the scaffold the crowd pressed round him.

One tottering old man with a long beard, his head completely bald, clutched him by the arm.

" Dost thou want aught with me, my friend ? " inquired Raleigh.

" My desire was to see thee, and to pray God for thee," the old man replied.

" I thank thee heartily, my good friend," said Raleigh. " Sorry I am that I stand in no case to return thee anything for thy good will. Yet, take this night-cap ; thou hast more need of it now than I have."

Nine o'clock was the hour of execution.

It wanted a few minutes to the hour, and the crowd was so dense that the guards had difficulty in piloting the victim to the platform.

Faint with sickness, Raleigh nevertheless mounted the steps briskly.

" Silence ! " roared a sheriff's officer. And when the murmuring had died down to a whisper, Raleigh began the usual farewell speech.

Never before or after that time did a valedictory oration stir an execution-mob to such depths of remorse.

He said that he intended to shout so that his words should reach my Lords Arundel, Northampton, and Doncaster, who were seated in a window some distance away.

"Do not do that," called Arundel, "we will come down to the scaffold."

They reached the steps, and Raleigh greeted them one by one, as if they were paying him a courtesy call at his house.

What was the offence which merited Raleigh's death ?

It is not at all clear. He had already suffered thirteen years' imprisonment for treason, a charge which was not proved. He was now being executed for the same old offence through the machinations of the Spanish ambassador. Though Raleigh was old and disease-ridden, the Spaniards were anxious to obtain their revenge for the defeats he had inflicted upon them.

On the scaffold Raleigh declared that the charges against him were untrue. Of the death of the Earl of Essex, he said :

> It doth make my heart to bleed to hear that such an imputation should be laid upon me ; for it is said that I was a prosecutor of the death of the Earl of Essex, and that I stood in a window over against him when he suffered in the Tower, and puffed out tobacco in disdain of him.
>
> I take God to witness that I had no hand in his blood, and was none of those that procured his death. I shed tears for him when he died ; and as I hope to look God in the face hereafter, my Lord of Essex did not see my face when he suffered, for I was afar off in the Armoury, where I saw him, but he saw not me.

This declaration was not quite true. It is known that Raleigh wrote a letter to Sir Robert Cecil urging him to "press Essex down," the inference being that Essex should be put to death. Whether it was intended by Raleigh to have this construction cannot be certain.

"My soul," continued Raleigh, "hath many times since been grieved that I was not nearer to him when he died ; because, as I understood afterwards, he asked for me at his death, to have been reconciled unto me."

It was a cold morning. The crowds huddled together for warmth. The prisoner on the scaffold looked pinched and ill.

" Let us defer the execution for a space," suggested the Sheriff of London, " and you can then come down and warm yourself."

" Nay, Mr Sheriff," replied Raleigh, " let us dispatch, for within this quarter of an hour mine ague will come upon me, and if I shall be not dead before then mine enemies will say that I quake for fear."

Raleigh knelt in prayer. Then, rising, he said, " I am going to God."

One by one he took leave of the assembled dignitaries and, in particular, the Earl of Arundel. He entreated the Earl to prevail upon King James to prevent any scandalous writing to defame him being published after his death.

With unfaltering steps he went to the block, picked up the axe, and felt its edge.

" This is a sharp medicine," he said, with a smile, " but it will cure all diseases."

He carefully adjusted his neck to the block.

" I will give the signal by raising my hand," he said to the executioner. " Fear not, but strike home ! "

He again laid himself down, and on being requested to alter the position of his head, remarked, " So the heart be right, it is no matter which way the head lies."

He gave the signal. The executioner hesitated.

" What dost thou fear ? " exclaimed Raleigh. " Strike, man ! "

In two blows the head of Sir Walter Raleigh rolled from the block. He was sixty-six.

Raleigh was born in 1552, and was educated at Oriel College, Oxford. Joining the volunteers, he was sent to assist the Queen of Navarre in defending the Protestants. Afterwards he served in the Low Countries against the Spaniards.

In 1578 he went on a voyage to the north-east coast of America. Returning to England, he helped in quelling an insurrection in Ireland, and was given as a reward a large estate in that country.

His rapid advancement is said to have been due to an act of gallantry in throwing his plush coat on the ground in order that Elizabeth might walk dry-shod over a patch of mud.

After a voyage to Newfoundland he offered to fit out an expedition to explore Florida. He returned before the winter and announced that he had discovered a land which had an excellent climate. He had taken possession of it in the name of the Queen. She named the new territory Virginia.

Raleigh was promoted to Captain of the Queen's Guard and Lieutenant-general of Cornwall. He fought against the Spanish Armada, and carried on a guerilla campaign against the Spanish possessions.

In 1588 he sent a fleet on a fifth voyage to Virginia, but in that year he gave up all his rights in the colony to a London concern.

In 1592 he fought against the Spaniards at Panama. In the following year he lost the Queen's favour temporarily through an intrigue with the daughter of Sir Nicholas Throckmorton, one of her maids of honour. Raleigh married her, and a few months later was restored to favour, receiving a grant of the manor of Sherborne in Dorset.

In 1595 Raleigh sailed for South America with a squadron of four ships for the conquest of Guiana. He occupied the city of San Joseph in Trinidad, and then sailed 400 miles up the river Orinoco.

But the lateness of the season compelled him to give up his plan of subduing Guiana.

In the following year he published an account of this expedition and was accused of exaggeration.

Next spring he collaborated with the Earl of Essex and Lord Effingham in the expedition against Cadiz, and in 1597 sailed with the same noblemen against the Azores, a project that was a failure owing to the ignorance of naval affairs of the Earl of Essex.

Raleigh was one of the principal opponents of Essex, and responsible in some measure for the tragic end of this royal favourite.

When Queen Elizabeth died, Raleigh's stock dropped. James I had his own favourites, particularly Lord Cecil, Sir Walter's enemy.

When Cecil made suggestions for the disposal of Raleigh, James agreed. Charges were brought against him of having been in communication with the King of Spain, and conspiring to make Lady Arabella Stuart queen of England.

The charges were not proved, but after a long trial he was found guilty.

He was remanded to the Tower. When the execution of the sentence was delayed, it gave hope to Lady Raleigh.

She called on the king, and pleaded for mercy.

But that arrogant son of the traitress Mary of Scotland and the ' gigolo ' Darnley replied harshly, " I maun have the land—I maun have it for Carr."

Thus did the indiscreet James expose his own hand. It was Raleigh's estates that he wanted.

Cecil, Earl of Salisbury died, and Raleigh made efforts for a reprieve.

Through the intervention of the Duke of Buckingham, Raleigh was liberated. He was sent on an expedition

to Guiana to obtain gold from a mine he had discovered
on his previous visit.   The expedition failed, and James
who had expected an extensive addition to his revenue
sent him back to the Tower.

The previous charges were revived, and although
Raleigh pleaded that everything had been remitted,
it was unavailing.

XVIII

Francis Bacon, Lord Chancellor—and "Broken Reed"

IT was a humble Lord Chancellor who awaited the deputation which had come to examine him on the question of accepting bribes. Francis Bacon had fallen low enough ; he could hardly fall lower.

They entered his room, not without pity ; not without the feeling that it might have happened to any one of them. Many of the prominent men of the days of James I had been guilty of the self-same corruption, even members of the deputation.

But Francis Bacon had committed the cardinal sin ; he had been found out.

" Do you acknowledge that your confession was given voluntarily ? " asked the leader.

Tears streamed from the eyes of the old man as he replied : " It is my act—my hand—my heart. Oh, my lords, spare a broken reed."

Bacon's degradation in many ways was analogous to that of Wolsey. Both had served their monarchs with fidelity ; both had enjoyed undisputed power ; both crashed at the zenith of their career.

But Bacon's punishment was tempered with mercy. Fined £40,000 and ordered to be confined in the Tower during the king's pleasure, debarred from holding office of State or in Parliament, and banished from within twelve miles of the Court, he was free within four days, the fine was remitted, and he was granted a general pardon, the censure of Parliament only remaining on record.

Bacon's fall from grace was due to his love of magnificence. He had an adequate income, but got heavily in debt.

Although in his later years he had £2500 a year, he died owing £22,000.

No words are more suitable than his own to illustrate the cause of his disgrace. One day, while his case was still proceeding at Westminster, he returned to his house and, as usual, the superbly dressed menials rose at his entrance. " Sit down, my masters," he said bitterly, " your rise has been my fall."

The years 1618–1621 had been crowded with incident for Bacon—his elevation to the Chancellorship, the publication of his *Novum Organum*, the unsurpassed magnificence of the festivities on his sixtieth birthday, and finally his impeachment.

Ben Jonson, who was present at the birthday celebrations, illustrated in verse the greatness of Bacon :

> England's High Chancellor, the destined heir,
> In his soft cradle, to his father's chair,
> Whose even thread the Fates spin round and full,
> Out of their choicest and their whitest wool.

A few months later Bacon was a discredited man. Compare the words of Jonson with those of Prince Charles, who, returning from a hunting expedition and espying a coach " attended with a goodly troop of horsemen," which he ascertained belonged to the late Lord Chancellor, exclaimed : " Well, do what we can, this man scorns to go out like snuff."

Had Bacon's life ended with the publication of his *Organum*, history would have had a more brilliant story to tell of him, but this work was barely finished when the rumours as to his integrity began to be circulated.

The Duke of Buckingham, who wanted the seals to be handed over to one of his own favourites, forced James to make an inquiry, and eventually twenty-eight charges of bribery and corruption were made against Bacon.

One of the cases concerned a man named Aubrey, who, having a suit in Chancery, had spent almost the whole of his fortune through the law's delays. He was advised by officers of the Court to make a present to the Lord Chancellor so that the wheels of process might revolve the more easily.

Unable to pay down the hundred pounds suggested at once, he obtained the money from a usurer. Unfortunately for both him and Bacon, he lost the case and immediately ventilated the whole matter.

The evidence against Bacon was too strong for a denial, and he admitted the offence. Asked to justify himself, he replied that the only justification he should make should be out of Job : " I have not hid my sin, as did Adam, nor concealed my faults in my bosom."

He threw himself upon the mercy of the court and added, " My humble desire is, that his Majesty would take the seals into his hands, which is a great downfall, and may serve, I hope, in itself, for an expiation of my faults."

After the scandal had died down, Bacon made attempts to regain his lost power by prayers to the king. He had always been a flatterer, and he said the most charming things about James and Prince Charles.

To the latter he hoped that as " his father the king had been his creator, so he, his son, would be his redeemer."

All fell upon ears that were deaf to his pleadings, and at last he was compelled to retire to the solitude of Gorhambury, his home near St Albans, where his father had built a beautiful mansion. There he gave himself up to literary work.

His own words, written to a friend, might serve as his epitaph : " I was the justest judge that was in England these fifty years ; but it was the justest censure in Parliament that was these two hundred years."

The last four years of his life were more useful to posterity than anything he had done in his high offices. In March, 1622, he presented to Prince Charles his *History of Henry VII*.

In the same year appeared *Historia Ventorum*, in January, 1623, *Historia Vitæ et Mortis*, and in October *De Augmentis Scientiarum*, while in December, 1624, he published his *Apophthegms* and *Translations of some of the Psalms*, and in 1625 an enlarged edition of his *Essays*.

Apart from his literary work, he had a scientific bent, and it was that which brought about his death. In March, 1626, he was on his way to London when it occurred to him that snow might be as great a preservative as salt.

He halted at a cottage in Highgate, bought a fowl, and stuffed it with snow. He contracted a sudden chill and, being unable to return home, was taken to the Earl of Arundel's home at Highgate.

The Earl was away, but his domestics, anxious to do all they possibly could for Bacon, put him to bed quickly between damp sheets.

In a few days he was dead, and left behind a letter to the Earl of Arundel, in which he said he was like the elder Pliny, " who had lost his life by trying an experiment about the burning of Mount Vesuvius."

He added that his experiment had "succeeded excellently well."

In his will he directed : "For my burial I desire it may be in St Michael's Church, St Albans ; there was my mother buried, and it is the parish church of my mansion house of Gorhambury, and it is the only Christian church within the walls of old Verulam."

The will also contained these words, "For my name and memory, I leave it to men's charitable speeches, to foreign nations, and the next ages."

A monument to his memory was erected by his faithful friend and secretary, Sir Thomas Meantys, who was himself buried at the feet of his master.

Bacon was one of the greatest orators of his time. He was successively member of Parliament for Melcombe Regis, Taunton, Liverpool, Middlesex, Southampton, Ipswich, St Albans, and the University of Cambridge.

As to his speeches there is the testimony of Ben Jonson :

> No man ever spake more neatly, more pressly, more weightily, or suffered less emptiness, less idleness in what he uttered.
> No member of his speech but consisted of its own graces. His hearers could not cough, or look aside from him without loss. He commanded where he spoke, and had his judges angry and pleased at his devotion.
> No man had their affections more in his power. The fear of every man that heard him was lest he should make an end.

Once, while Attorney-General, Bacon admitted to the king that during one of his cases his voice served him well for two hours and a half, and not one of his auditors who was present at the beginning of the speech left the court until he had finished.

Even Coke, the Lord Chancellor, who was no admirer of Bacon, could not help saying that "it was a famous argument."

Bacon was born on January 22, 1561, at York House, London. His father, Sir Nicholas Bacon, held the Great Seal with the title of Lord Keeper throughout a greater part of the first half of the reign of Elizabeth.

He was educated at home and at Trinity College, Cambridge. He was returned for Parliament in 1584, and in 1593 the Earl of Essex endeavoured to obtain for him the office of Attorney-General.

But Essex was generally disliked, and the office went to Coke. He then tried to prevail upon Elizabeth to give Bacon the office of Solicitor-General vacated by Coke, with no better success.

Coke seems to have been Bacon's rival in most things, even for the hand of the beautiful Lady Hatton. It was fortunate for Bacon that Coke forestalled him, for she proved to be rather a handful for Coke.

In January, 1597, he made his first appearance as an author with the first part of his *Essays*, but in September of the same year was arrested for debt at the instance of a moneylender, and placed in a sponging-house.

In the meantime he had received from Elizabeth various small grants of land, including the rectory and church of Cheltenham.

He was responsible in great measure for the result of the prosecution of Lord Essex, his former friend, who was executed for treason.   Bacon, in a letter of apology, declared that, as a public servant, he had no option but to endeavour to secure Essex's conviction.

While Queen Elizabeth lived Bacon received no public appointment, but on the coronation of James I he was, at the age of forty-two, one of the many knights created by the new king.

At the age of forty-six he was made Solicitor-General.   In 1611 he was made a judge, and two years later Attorney-General.

In 1617 he received the seals as Lord Keeper, and next year became Lord Chancellor, being made Lord Verulam. He was advanced to the rank of Viscount St Albans a few days after he celebrated his sixtieth birthday.

XIX

The Mystery of Shakespeare and Anne

I give unto my wife my second-best bed, with the furniture.

THIS strange phrase in the will of William Shakespeare has provided a problem.

Shakespeare originally drew up the will without a mention of his wife. The " second-best bed " was an afterthought inserted in a few lines.

The will makes bequests to his daughter Judith (Mrs Quiney), his daughter Susanna (Mrs Hall), his sister, Joan Hart, her three sons, William, Thomas, and Michael, and to a number of friends and acquaintances at Stratford.

The theory has been advanced that it was a common practice at the time for a testator to specify in his will a bequest of a certain piece of furniture to his wife.

A bedstead was often named. It was not unusual for the best bed to go to another member of the family, leaving the wife the second-best.

On the other hand, there is other evidence to show that Shakespeare was determined to dispossess his wife. In common law a widow was entitled to a third of the value of freehold estate for life, but the poet had already prevented the usual process of law by barring the dower in connexion with his purchase of his freehold estate at Blackfriars.

It has been suggested that Shakespeare specified the second-best bed because Anne preferred it to any other. Another theory is that the best bed was attached to the panelling of the wall of the bed-chamber, and was not portable.

A house at Blackfriars referred to in the will was in the parish of St Anne. He bequeathed it to his daughter, Susanna Hall. In the deed of conveyance the house is described as

> abutting upon a street leading down to Puddle Wharf, and now late in the tenure or occupation of one William Ireland, part of which said tenement is erected over a great gate leading to a capital messuage, which some time was in the tenure of William Blackwell, Esq., deceased, and since then in the tenure or occupation of the Right Honourable Henry, now Earl of Northumberland.

The original deed of conveyance was placed in the City of London Library.

So few facts concerning the early life of Shakespeare have come to light that it is not surprising that Anne Hathaway herself is a somewhat vague person.

At Stratford-on-Avon is preserved the cottage in which she lived, but documentary evidence substantiating her connexion with Shakespeare is rather meagre.

Shakespeare was eighteen and Anne about twenty-six when the couple were married.

To Nicholas Rowe, the first modern editor of Shakespeare, belongs the credit for discovering the name of Shakespeare's wife. He gave the name as Hathaway, while Joseph Greene later succeeded in tracing her to a family of that name living in Shottery, one of the hamlets of Stratford.

It was about the year 1582 that Shakespeare and Anne were married. She is believed to have been identical with the daughter Agnes mentioned in the will of Richard Hathaway of Shottery, who died in 1581, while in possession of the farmhouse known as " Anne Hathaway's Cottage."

Though Agnes as a name was distinct from Anne, there is reason to believe that the latter was a corruption of the former.

On November 28, 1582, a bond of marriage was executed. This was brought to light in 1833 by Sir Thomas Phillips, and was obtained from the registry at Worcester.

There is no documentary evidence of a church ceremony. The bond is signed by two husbandmen, Fulk Sandells and John Richardson, who

bind themselves in £40 for the security of the bishop on his granting licence for the solemnization of marriage between William Shagspere and Anne Hathaway with only once asking of the bannes.

The conditions expressed therein are as follows :

That if hereafter there shall not appere any lawfull lett or impediment by reason of any precontract, consanguinitie, affinitie, or by any other lawfull means whatsoever, but that William Shagspere, the one partie, and Anne Hathwey, of Stratford, in the dioces of Worcester, Maiden, may lawfully solemnize matrimony together, and in the same afterwards remaine and continew like man and wife, according unto the laws in that behalf provided : and moreover if there be not at this present time any action, sute, quarrel or demaund, moved or depending before any judge, ecclesiastical or temporal, for and concerning any suche lawfull lett or impediment : and, moreover, if the said William Shagspere do not proceed to solemnize of marriage with the said Anne Hathwey, without the consent of her frinds : and also if the said William do upon his owne proper costs and expenses defend and save harmles the Right Reverend Father in God, Lord John Bushop of Worcester, and his offycers, for licensing them, the said William and Anne, to be married together with once asking of the bannes of matrimony between them, and for all other causes which may ensue by reason or occasion thereof ; that then the said obligation to be void and of none effect, or els to stand and abide in full force and virtue.

8

It has been suggested that the procedure of " once asking of the bannes " was due to a reluctance on the part of the young bridegroom, who might have realized the gravity of the step he was taking if he heard the banns called on more than one occasion.

On the other hand, the solution is no doubt to be found in the fact that Mrs Shakespeare presented her husband with their first child on May 26, 1583, just six months after the date of the marriage contract.

The marriage, too, was near the date of Advent during which ceremonies were never solemnized. The only procedure by banns would have resulted in a delay until January.

It may also have been connected with the fact that under date of January 12, 1578–9, there is a mysterious entry in the marriage register at Stratford of " William Wilsonne " and " Anne Hathaway of Shotterye."

There is no record of Anne's baptism, for she was born before any religious registers were kept, so that her age at her death can only be confirmed from her monument, which gives it as sixty-seven in 1623.

It was a strange circumstance, too, that on the day before the contract was executed, an entry was made in the bishop's register of the issue of a licence for the marriage between William Shakespeare and " Annam Whateley de Temple Grafton."

This may refer to the Hathaway marriage ; if so, there has evidently been a mistake in setting down the name of the bride. Temple Grafton may have been the place of residence of Anne, but there are no registers for Temple Grafton.

The facts of the story of Anne Hathaway and her relation to Shakespeare can only be one of conjecture.

It is certain, however, that the first offspring of the marriage, Susanna, was born in May, 1583. A boy and girl, twins, named Hamnet and Judith, were baptized on February 2, 1585.

Shakespeare's will was drafted in January, 1616, by Francis Collins, a solicitor at Warwick. It was finally executed two months later. Next month, according to that gossiper, John Ward, vicar of the town in Charles II's time, Shakespeare entertained two literary friends, the famous Ben Jonson and Michael Drayton.

It is suggested by the vicar that at this function Shakespeare " drank too hard " and " died in a feavour there contracted."

It is believed that the poet's death took place on April 23, 1616, he having just completed his fifty-second year. Two days later he was buried in the chancel of Stratford Church in front of the altar.

To prevent his bones being taken to the charnel-house of the churchyard, as was often the custom, he directed that the following should be inscribed on his tombstone :

> Good friend, for Jesus' sake forbeare
> To dig the dust enclosed heare ;
> Bleste be the man that spares these stones,
> And curst be he that moves my bones.

A monument was designed by a Southwark tomb-maker, and affixed to the north wall of the chancel with a device which claims that Shakespeare was the greatest man of letters of his age, whom other contemporary writers were merely fit to serve as " page " or menial.

It is not surprising that there has been much controversy concerning Shakespeare's authorship of the plays and poems, seeing that the only authentic relics of Shakespeare's handwriting are six signatures attached to legal documents.

No lifetime-portrait of Shakespeare is known, though two were produced after his death.

The truth is that England's greatest bard is surrounded with a halo of mystery.

Over a thousand books have been written to prove either that Will Shakespeare of Stratford was not William Shakespeare the poet and dramatist, or that the works attributed to Shakespeare were really written by Bacon or others.

An American writer, J. C. Hart, has said that Shakespeare's authorship is impossible. The theory that Bacon was the author also arose in America.

Certainly there are many problems concerning Shakespeare that are still unsolved, such as the date of his birth, his life to the age of eighteen, and the date and place of his marriage.

XX

" CRACK-BRAINED " WILLIAM HARVEY

" CRACK-BRAINED?" was the description applied to William Harvey, the discoverer of the circulation of the blood, when he first propounded his theories.

Only Charles I, whose sagacity could not always be questioned, and who was a firm friend to a loyal servant, stood by Harvey when the medical profession of both England and the Continent were trying to discredit the man. The usual accusation was made that Harvey was propagating doctrines which tended to subvert the authority of Holy Scripture. Harvey was a quack—they said—a lunatic, a person unfit to hold medical degrees.

But, through all the persecution, Charles refused to take any part. He said little, perhaps—he was otherwise engaged—but he refused to give way to the demands that Harvey should be deprived of his position as King's physician.

Between the King and Harvey there was an affection which showed itself in a remarkable way when the first great battle of the Civil War was fought at Edgehill.

Harvey was a non-combatant, but he had courage.

" Look after the Princes," said Charles. " They must come to no harm. You are one of the few I can trust."

An old chronicler says :

> During the fight the Prince and Duke of York were committed to his care. He withdrew with them under a hedge and took out a book and read.

117

But he had not read very long before a bullet of a great gun grazed on the ground near him, which made him remove his station.

Harvey was small, with a choleric temper.

In person [the historian proceeds] he was of the lowest stature, round-faced, olive as to complexion, little eye, round, very black, full of spirit ; his hair black as a raven. In his younger days he wore a dagger, as the fashion then was, which he would be apt to draw out on every occasion.

During the controversy which raged about his theory, however, he preserved an unruffled dignity.

Harvey was the eldest son of Thomas Harvey, yeoman, and was born at Folkestone in 1578. He was educated at Canterbury Grammar School and Gonville and Caius College at Cambridge.

He went to the Continent to study physics. While he was at the University of Padua it began to dawn upon him that the accepted theories regarding the blood were wrong.

In 1604 he married, and five years later was appointed physician to St Bartholomew's Hospital.

His ability attracted attention, and in a short time he was appointed physician to several noblemen, including the Earl of Arundel and Lord Chancellor Bacon.

Harvey first began to lecture on the action of the heart and the motion of the blood in 1615. Thirteen years later he put his views on paper at Frankfurt. Up to this time only a few of his associates were aware of his discoveries, but when his theories were published they were followed by hundreds of treatises by his rivals who tried to contravene his theories.

Keen attempts were made in England to discredit the physician, and his practice declined. On the Continent he was turned down with contempt.

While the controversy was going on, Charles I appointed Harvey his physician, although his general ability as a medical man was also being questioned.

The King was often an interested spectator of Harvey's experiments.

Harvey preserved a discreet silence, and allowed the clamour to simmer down.

A few years later he accompanied the Earl of Arundel and Surrey, Lord Marshal of England, in his travels abroad.

At Vienna, Harvey would often disappear for the greater part of the day. When inquiries were made, they would find him in the woods investigating strange trees and plants. He was discouraged from continuing these wanderings, for there was danger of thieves and wild beasts.

During the Civil War, Harvey followed Charles throughout his campaign, and was at Oxford while the headquarters of the King were located there. In 1645 he was made Warden of Merton College, and became friendly with Dr Bathurst of Trinity.

Together they studied the problem of incubation, Bathurst having a number of sitting hens in his bedroom.

On the surrender of Oxford in 1646, Harvey returned to London, and went to live with his brother, Eliab, at a house in Poultry, London, and then retired to a house at Coombe, Surrey.

When his blood-theories were first publicly demonstrated at Vienna by Harvey, thirty years after they had been published, he won over many of the scientists who were still opposed to his views.

In his retirement Harvey was visited by Dr Ent, a close friend, who gives a pen-picture of the man in repose.

" I found him," says Ent, " in his retirement, not far from town, with a sprightly and cheerful countenance, investigating, like Democritus, the nature of things."

Asked if all were well with him, Harvey replied :

> How can that be when the State is so agitated with storms, and I myself am kept in the open sea ?
>
> And, indeed, were not my mind solaced by my studies, and the recollections of the observations I have formerly made, there is nothing which should make me desirous of a longer continuance.
>
> But, thus employed, this obscure life and vacation from public cares which disquiet other minds is the medicine of mine.

In 1653 Harvey presented the College of Physicians with a library and museum, and in the following year he was made President of the College, but declined the office on account of advancing years.

Harvey had been a careful man.   Out of his practice before the Civil War he had saved £20,000.

In 1651, Ent tried to induce him to publish the result of his further researches.   But, referring to his previous experiences with *Exercises of the Heart*, he said :

> Would you be the man to have me quit the peaceful haven where I now pass my life and launch again upon the faithless sea ? . . .
>
> Much better is it oftentimes to grow wise at home than, by publishing what you have gathered with infinite pains, to stir up tempests that may rob you of peace and quiet for the rest of your days.

At last Harvey was persuaded, and his researches were published. They did not bring condemnation ; they enhanced his reputation.

Harvey was now regarded as the most distinguished physician of his age. A statue was erected to commemorate him in the hall of the College of Physicians, but this was destroyed in the Great Fire of 1666.

Aubrey, his biographer, writes :

His piety was not less remarkable than his genius.

Throughout his works he delights to give expression to his sense of the power and goodness of the Creator.

He saw in all things the hands of God, not only in their creation but in their preservation ; and he held that the Almighty does not work by general laws alone, but by special providence, which controls and actuates all things both great and small.

He thus agreed with Cicero that even from the perfect structure of bees and ants the perfection of the Almighty God might be inferred.

And he maintained that all creatures exist through a present God, their Creator and Father, without whose divine power nothing can be.

Harvey was the first physiologist who appreciated the relations between the highest and the lowest of organized beings, and who used the simplicity of construction in the one to explain the complexity of structure in the other.

Until Harvey wrote, the liver was regarded as the origin of the veins, which were alone believed to be the proper blood-vessels. The arteries, it was thought, were channels for air or vital spirits, with which a little blood was accidentally mixed.

XXI

GALILEO, STAR-GAZER

ONE of the most pathetic incidents in history was the appearance of the aged Galileo, clothed in sackcloth, before the Inquisition in June, 1633.

Upon his knees, before the array of cardinals, he swore by the Bible to recant his heretical teachings regarding the earth's motion, and was required to repeat the seven penitential psalms weekly for three years.

But his recantation did not alter the fact that he had made one of the most important astronomical discoveries of all time, and scientists all over the world were able to continue unmolested the researches which Galileo had begun.

He was taken to the prisons of the Inquisition, but the Church was satisfied with his renunciation. He was released after four days.

It was an intolerant age, when the Church assumed a sovereign right over the persons of its adherents.

Galileo Galilei was born at Pisa on February 18, 1564. He had noble antecedents, but his parents were poor, and he received his first education at the monastery of Vallombrosa, near Florence.

He learned Greek and Latin, became a logician, and showed aptitude for mechanical invention.

There was little in his inclinations to suggest on what lines he would develop, for he was also a skilful musician and showed a taste for painting.

Sitting in the cathedral of Pisa, when seventeen years old, Galileo observed a curious, but hitherto unnoticed, phenomenon in connexion with the hanging lamp which was swinging backward and forward.

Whatever the range of its oscillations, he noticed that each movement was completed in the same period of time.

Startled by this discovery, he subjected it to verification and ascertained definitely that the swing of a pendulum always took an equal time whether it covered a large or small range.

Up to this time his father had hoped that he would adopt a medical career. Himself a mathematician, he saw little in the ability of Galileo which implied that he would follow in his father's footsteps, but an accident changed the whole tenor of Galileo's career.

Overhearing a lesson in geometry, his interest was awakened, and with his father's permission he began to study science and mathematics. He applied himself diligently to his studies, but before he could obtain a degree, the poverty of his father caused his withdrawal from the university, and he returned to Florence.

For a time he lectured at the Florentine Academy, and at the age of twenty-two he invented the hydrostatic balance and published an essay describing the discovery.

All Italy, if not the world, soon began to hear of the young scientist of Pisa, and on the suggestion of his former patron, the Marchese Guidubaldo del Monte of Pesaro, a well-known scientist, he wrote a work on the centre of gravity on solids, which brought him the post at Pisa University as a lecturer.

The next two years he spent in researches into dynamics and was able to establish the first principles. He was able to show that bodies of different weights fell with the same velocity, his experiments being conducted from the leaning Tower of Pisa, and also demonstrated that a projectile described a parabola in its path.

Galileo's precocity was somewhat annoying to the elder scientists, and his sarcasm was rather cutting, so that he was not always as popular as he might have been.

Eventually, through prejudice, he was compelled to resign his professorship, and he went to Florence. In 1592 he was appointed to the chair of mathematics at Padua, where he remained until 1610, his salary being progressively increased.

He had long believed in the theory of Copernicus regarding the solar system. This is instanced by a letter to Kepler in 1597, but fear of ridicule prevented his acknowledging the fact.

In the spring of 1609, Galileo, while at Venice, heard of a curious instrument which had been invented by a certain Hans Lippershey, of Middleburg, and which, it was said, enabled objects at a distance to be seen more clearly.

Whether he actually investigated Lippershey's invention is not known, but he began to experiment on similar lines.

He obtained two spectacle-glasses, one convex on one side and the other concave on one side. Placing these at opposite ends of a tube, and applying his eye to the concave glass, he found objects magnified and brought nearer.

He quickly improved on this first attempt and was soon able to produce a telescope which magnified thirty times. He made hundreds of these instruments, which were sold all over the world, and this type is now used as opera glasses.

He then began observations on the moon, and discovered its surface to be irregular, and in January, 1610, he found Jupiter to be accompanied by four satellites.

Naturally, all these discoveries created a sensation.

As a result of them the Grand Duke of Tuscany gave him a high salary.

He went on from triumph to triumph, ascertaining the crescent form of Venus, spots on the sun, and the curious rings of Saturn, all of which was by no means to the taste of his scientific contemporaries.

Aristotle was good enough for them, and they would not believe that many centuries-old theories could be abandoned.

One of the philosophers declared that he " would never grant that Italian his new stars, though he should die for it." Although Galileo was able to prove all his assertions, his appeals to common sense were all in vain, and philosophers of his own order were definitely hostile.

The discovery of Jupiter's moons was a confirmation of the theory of Copernicus, and was received triumphantly by its advocates.

It was probably a bad move on the part of Galileo to go to Rome to exhibit his telescope. Although he met with a flattering reception at the Papal Court, it was this which induced him to write his *Letters on the Solar Spots* (1613), in which he advocated the Copernican theory.

Studying this work closely, the Church authorities discovered what appeared to be discrepancies between Galileo's view of the solar system and that propounded by the Scriptures.

At first the controversy took the form of mild discussion, but Galileo became somewhat impetuous and began to ram home his theories to the annoyance of the authorities.

The movement against Galileo which followed was by no means a unanimous one, for the Church had taken no cognizance of the theories of Copernicus, and if he had acted more discreetly there is little doubt that Galileo would have escaped the indignity to which he was subjected.

It is believed that a diatribe against him by a preacher from the pulpit induced him to cross swords with the Church. At all events, he was brought before the Inquisition at Rome in February, 1615, where he solemnly renounced all his previous doctrines and gave an undertaking not to teach them.

Three months later he returned to Florence, by no means upset with his admonition by Pope Paul V. Nevertheless, for the next seven years he lived in retirement and continued his researches.

At the end of that period Galileo broke silence with his *Saggiatore*, dealing with the nature of comets. This was printed at Rome in October, 1623, and was dedicated to the new Pope, Urban VIII. Although there was in it a suggestion of Copernicus, it was received with acclamation by both ecclesiastical and lay authorities.

Galileo's next move was an attempt to obtain the revocation of the decree of 1616 in view of the attitude of the Church which seemed favourable and the pressure brought upon him by his friends.

But instead of approaching the Church authorities, he brought out a new work which was regarded as a defiance of the edict of sixteen years before.

Though the production brought Galileo applause from all parts of Europe, the Church soon began to take action. At the end of August, 1632, the sale was prohibited, and in October the author was ordered to appear before the Inquisition at Rome.

Although he pleaded bad health and age the authorities would listen to no excuses, and in February of the following year he arrived in Rome and was detained until June, when he was examined by the Inquisition, and threatened with torture which it was never really intended to carry out.

On the following day he recanted, and received the punishment already mentioned. On July 6 he was allowed to depart for Siena, where he spent several months in the house of the archbishop, who was one of his numerous friends.

In December he returned to Florence and spent the remaining eight years of his life at his villa at Arcetri. Through his telescope he made a further discovery regarding the moon.

He died on January 8, 1642, following a fever which he suddenly contracted while discussing his theories with two of his pupils.

XXII

RENÉ DESCARTES, THE GREAT PSYCHOLOGIST

RENÉ DESCARTES (or Des Cartes), one of the world's greatest philosophers, met a premature death through the caprice of a queen.

The Queen of Sweden was a powerful woman in the best of health. She could not understand the weakness of others, and when she insisted on pursuing her philosophical studies at five o'clock every morning, she did not realize that her tutor, Descartes, was gradually dying from consumption.

Descartes's delicate health had been further undermined by the worry caused by his persecution on account of his writings. Like Galileo, and many others who have made great contributions to science and philosophy, Descartes had to put up with the opposition of the Church.

He was born in Touraine of Breton parents on March 31, 1596.

He had a consumptive mother who died a few days after his birth, and there seemed every probability that the young Descartes would die at an early age.

Like Sir Isaac Newton, who was a weakly child and not expected to live beyond infancy, Descartes picked up in health, and was able to be educated like a normal child.

He was sent to the Jesuit College at La Flèche until he was sixteen, and astonished the professors with his knowledge, often taking exception to some of their conclusions.

DESCARTES AT HIS DESK

This illustration appears as the frontispiece to Descartes' *Epistolæ Omnes* (Frankfurt, 1692)   128

By his eighth year he had gained the title of the young philosopher, through his anxiety to learn and his constant questioning.

The Jesuits took a delight in their pupil, but when he left their college he declared that he " had derived no other benefit from his studies than that of a conviction of his utter ignorance, and a profound contempt for the systems of philosophy in vogue."

He appears to have had a contempt for his professors, whom he never thought of thanking for their pains. This is his own opinion of the teaching of his day :

> As soon as my age permitted me to quit my preceptors, I entirely gave up the study of letters ; and resolving to seek no other science than that which I could find in myself, or else in the great book of the world, I employed the remainder of my youth in travel.

His father sent him to Paris to broaden his outlook, but there he fell in with a loose set, and gave himself up to dissipation and pleasure.

He had almost sunk to irretrievable depths when he was rescued by his friend Father Mersenne, who induced him to recommence his studies.

But his associates pursued him, and he had to hide in a remote corner of Paris to escape their attentions. Meanwhile he continued his studies of mathematics and philosophy.

Emerging from his hiding with an intellect sharpened by solitude and with considerably increased learning, he was alarmed to find that his family were preparing for him to enter on a military career.

At first he refused to accede to their suggestions, and was persuaded only when he was convinced that a more active life for a time would be beneficial to his health.

Personal experience, too, he argued with himself,

9

would enable him to grasp the deeper problems of life
more than all the theorizing.

He went to Holland and served under Prince Maurice
as a volunteer. This, however, was not active enough
for him, for military operations had been suspended for
a time.

So he gave up his commission in the French Army
and joined the Bavarians, taking part in the Thirty
Years' War, in which he distinguished himself.

In 1622, after five years' military service, he returned
to France and finally gave up his profession of arms.
Most military men of his day took part in the prevailing
political quarrels, but Descartes would never lend himself
to anything of the kind. He studied the question quietly
from another angle—the point of view of human passions.

The death of his mother left him enough money to
live on, and gradually he obtained fame as a mathematician and philosopher. This notoriety was little to
his taste, particularly as his writing incurred the hostility
of the Church.

He was criticized severely by men of influence, and
he decided to leave his country. At the age of thirty-
three he went to Holland and hid himself, not even
allowing his friends to know where he was.

After eight years, he produced in 1637 his world-
famous book the *Discourse on Method*. Later he published
a successor called *Meditations*, upon which he asked for
criticism. The two works made his name famous all
over Europe, but the Dutch theologians were roused
against him, and looking round for another country to
live in, he gave way to the request of the Queen of Sweden
that he should go there.

Descartes was the greatest champion of the value of
reason in solving the problems which had usually been
left to faith. The Church declared that it was necessary

to believe in God. Descartes, on the other hand, declared that reason could prove it.

He was a great master of the art of deduction. For anything he observed he attempted to find a reason. He was one of the greatest mathematicians of all time.

Descartes did not agree with the teaching of the schools and he advocated a completely new start. He discarded all books, and proceeded to argue that " whatever is clearly and distinctly thought must be true."

From this he evolved the idea of a " Perfect Being," on the ground that we, being imperfect, could visualize perfection and, therefore, perfection must exist.

There can be no question, Descartes argues, that there exists in our own minds the idea of an All-perfect Being. That being the case, how did such a conception originate ?

We cannot manufacture ideas out of nothing. Neither can they come from a finite being or from the finite world around us. They can only come from the Infinite Being himself who answers to the ideal in our thoughts.

Thus we have a psychological proof of the existence of God.

The philosophy of Descartes should have been the death-blow of atheism. Here is a little essay on the First Cause which the most expert logician cannot dismiss with impunity. It is put in as simple language as possible :

> My existence is not self-caused, but is derived from some cause outside myself. The source cannot be in an object around me, nor is it from my parents, for I cannot come from a less perfect source than my own ideas, that is, less perfect than God.

Descartes proceeds to prove the existence of God by mathematics, and having satisfied himself that there is a God, he deals with His character, and declares that the human mind, in all its deeper movements, becomes the simple instrument of the Divine will.

Everything in creation is passive. Every single thing in the universe is brought into being by the exertion of the Divine power and will. If not sustained by the same creative power it would fall of existence.

Shoals of works have been written on the philosophy of Descartes, and some of his conclusions have been proved false, to the satisfaction of later philosophers.

His idea is a universe which is a machine kept in motion simply by the Divine power.

From these conclusions it is easy to draw others that are obviously erroneous. It presupposes, for instance, that man has not free will, and that animals are automatons.

Despite the danger of false conclusions from Descartes' philosophy, however, he must be given credit as the great pioneer of all modern psychology.

Descartes had some remarkable theories in the realm of physics which are known to be wrong in these days. He regarded the heavens as a vast fluid mass revolving round the sun, a theory which was considerably in advance of his day, but which was not of course true.

There is no doubt, however, that his theories formed a basis from which Newton could begin.

Descartes had not been in the employ of the Queen of Sweden for more than a year when he died.

Sweden had a climate vastly unlike that of his native Touraine. Moreover, his work at the Court necessitated giving up many of his old habits, the sudden change being detrimental to his weak constitution.

His death occurred in 1650 in the fifty-fourth year of his age.

XXIII

ROBERT BLAKE, THE DARE-DEVIL

IT was a good thing for Britain that Sir Henry Savile, Warden of Merton College, disliked short men.

When Robert Blake competed for a fellowship, with the intention of devoting himself to learning, he was unsuccessful because of the curious fad of the warden.

Nevertheless, young Blake took the degree of Master of Arts and remained at Oxford for nine years.

When Blake was twenty-five, his father, Humphrey, who had speculated unwisely, recalled his son to his home at Bridgwater, Somerset, and Robert had to attend to the family affairs. Not long afterwards he followed his father's coffin to the churchyard.

The widow, left with a numerous family, looked to Robert for support.

Thus Robert Blake became one of the greatest military geniuses England has ever produced.

When he took up the cause of Parliament against the King, he it was who saved the situation when a victory for the King's armies would have turned the whole country against Parliament.

About the year 1640, Blake was a member of the Short Parliament for Bridgwater. He became a member of the Long Parliament in 1645, when the issue between Parliament and King had become defined.

Three years before Blake had seen how matters were drifting. In 1642 he began to collect arms in the West Country.

His first prominent appearance was at the siege of Bristol in 1643.

Blake was in charge of one of the forts called Prior's Hill. When Prince Rupert, Charles's commander, appeared before the city and began the assault, he found Prior's Hill a problem.

In an attempt to pass this stronghold, Rupert found that his every advance was taken in flank by the steady fire of Blake's men.

Time after time the column advanced, but had to fall back before Blake's resolute defence. He had given orders to his men to pick off the officers of Rupert's army, and down they went like a row of skittles.

At last the King's forces took to flight. Out rushed Blake and pursued them.

But Colonel Fiennes began to parley with the Cavaliers after Blake had cleared the hill. He agreed to surrender the city to Rupert, and thus Blake's efforts were in vain.

Blake became Lieutenant-colonel of Popham's regiment, in command of 1500 picked men. He attacked Bridgwater, and while there he learned that his brother Samuel had been killed in a foolish expedition in search of a Royalist officer.

" Sam was a fool. He had no business there," said Blake. But, whatever he thought of his brother, he did not neglect Sam's children. He took them for his own, and they looked upon him as their father.

The war dragged on until the winter of 1644–5, when the King might have finished the strife once and for all with one victorious battle.

The Royalist army attacked Taunton, in which Blake was isolated.

Charles had decided upon the capture of Taunton, because the town was interfering with the transport of supplies to the West.

They summoned Blake with threats of fire and sword.

"Last drop of our blood," said Blake, without attempting to parley.

They tried to storm him out and to starve him out.

"Eat my boots first," said Blake.

"Why don't you storm him out?" said the West-country supporters of the King.

"Batter him out," advised Goring, one of the Cavalier commanders.

"I'll have him out," said Sir Richard Greville, and swore he would never leave the place until he did.

A rash vow.

Month after month passed, and the success so necessary to the Cavaliers did not materialize. They could not get Blake out of Taunton.

In the meantime Cromwell had raised an army, and four regiments were sent to the relief of Taunton. Obsessed with the capture of the town, the King decided to make another attack. The battle of Naseby intervened, and the King's army was destroyed.

Had Blake failed to hold Taunton it would have released a large army for the King's campaign elsewhere. He had held Taunton for a year and withstood two great sieges.

The second phase of Blake's career was as a seaman. The English Navy was of little account before Blake's time. It was composed of a miserable collection of vessels, badly prepared for war purposes.

On July 12, 1648, the fleet mutinied. Eleven ships under Admiral Batten sailed to Holland to Prince Charles. The Prince, hoping that the rest of the Navy would join his colours, came over with the squadron and anchored in the Downs.

The Prince's ships and the Commonwealth Navy faced each other.

Cromwell, alarmed, called in Blake and two other military officers, Colonels Deane and Topham, to command the Navy.

Blake was nearly fifty, and was called sea-general.

With his squadron he undertook to attack Rupert, who had now established his headquarters at Kinsale in Ireland while carrying on a system of marauding. Blake blockaded Rupert, who escaped with seven ships to Portugal.

Blake pursued Rupert, and when King John of Portugal declared for Prince Charles, he seized the Brazil fleet coming out of the river Tagus, and later the South American fleet coming home laden with rich merchandise.

The Portuguese had had enough, and advised Rupert to sail. He slipped from the Tagus into the Mediterranean, and at Carthagena Blake caught some of the ships and destroyed them.

Blake was the first English admiral who had appeared in the Mediterranean since the Crusades.

In about eighteen months Blake returned home, was made Warden of the Cinque Ports, and received the thanks of Parliament as well as a donation of £1000.

Next Blake subdued the Scilly Isles, which had been fortified by the Royalists. His next service was the conquest of the Channel Islands.

The war against the Dutch began in the summer of 1652 with battles in the English Channel. In November Van Tromp, the Dutch admiral, caught Blake in the Downs and gave him a beating, the Englishman being compelled to seek refuge in the Thames.

This decided Blake to reform the Navy. He soon had his new fleet, and in February, 1653, went after Van Tromp, who had gone down the Channel with a broom at his masthead in token of his intention to sweep the seas.

On February 18 he found Van Tromp at Rochelle. With his own flagship, the *Triumph*, he led the way into the battle.

The battle was fought near Portland, with all the forces that the English and Dutch could command. On the first day the English destroyed eight ships. On the second day there was a running fight up Channel.

On the third Blake forced Van Tromp into Calais roads, and in the night the Dutch admiral escaped to Holland with remnants of his fleet.

The English took about fifty ships, including merchantmen, and caused the rest of the Continent to shiver with apprehension.

A number of smaller battles followed. In the final encounter between the two commonwealths Van Tromp was shot through the heart.

In 1657 Blake achieved his most spectacular victory by destroying a Spanish squadron in the port of Teneriffe.

War had been declared against Spain, and when the Admiral heard that the Spanish fleet lay at anchor in the Bay of Santa Cruz, he entered with twenty-five ships.

The defences included a castle on the north and seven other forts at various points. The Spanish Navy was drawn up under the guns of the castle, an apparently impregnable position.

Blake posted some of his ships to fire upon the fortification and himself attacked the galleons. Though the smallest of the ships were larger than any of the English, the Spaniards were compelled to abandon them one after the other.

The forts and smaller vessels were battered and forsaken, and the whole fleet was set on fire.

When the news reached England the military experts were amazed. It was argued that no one in his right senses would have dared to attempt the feat.

The Spaniards consoled themselves with the belief that they had fought devils and not men.

After cruising about for some time, Blake set sail for home. As his ship was entering Plymouth Sound on August 7, 1657, he died. His body was embalmed, and after lying in state at Greenwich was buried in Westminster Abbey.

XXIV

CROMWELL SHOWS HIS TEETH

WHEN Oliver Cromwell strutted into the House of Commons and, turning to the fifty-three members of the Long Parliament, cried : " Be gone, you rogues ; you have sat long enough," he was not quite so polite as Charles I had been on an earlier and almost analogous occasion, when he demanded that the five members should be handed over to him for punishment.

There was a temperamental difference between the two men. Charles, standing by his " Divine Right," was a more dignified character than the brusque yeoman, Cromwell.

Cromwell's righteous indignation was supported by force. Charles believed in his own personality, and although he, too, had his followers behind him, he could not conceive that the Commons should refuse any demand of their king.

The King had delivered an oration, carefully worded and full of arrogance. Cromwell let flow a string of invective that made the parliamentary limpets squirm.

The members of the Long Parliament were busy trying to dig themselves in when Cromwell appeared so suddenly. They were debating a Bill providing for the future representation of Parliament in which they themselves would have permanent seats.

Followed by a company of musketeers, Cromwell entered the Chamber, according to one report, in plain black clothes and grey worsted stockings, and quietly took his seat.

For a time he listened to their arguments, his anger rising. Then, when the Speaker was about to put the motion, he said to Harrison, his chief officer, " Now is the time—I must do it."

He jumped to his feet, threw his plumed hat on to a seat, and began to talk to them.

" We have had enough of this," he said. " I will put an end to your prating."

He recovered his hat, placed it back on his head with a flourish, and strode on to the floor of the House, ignoring the remonstrating hand of Harrison.

The members were " deniers of justice and oppressors," he declared, and he charged them with entering into a secret arrangement with the Presbyterians.

Sir Harry Vane was the only member who had courage to resist Cromwell. He characterized his language as unparliamentary.

" I know it," shouted the dictator, as he strode up and down, pointing a finger of scorn at first one and then another of those present.

> It is not fit that you should sit here any longer. You have sat too long for any good you have been doing lately. You shall now give place to better men.

He continued to pace up and down the floor, glaring first at one member and then at another. " Call them in ! " he ordered Harrison, and a file of soldiers entered the House.

Continuing his rapid striding, he went on : " You are no Parliament ! Some of you are drunkards "—he shook his fist at Chaloner—" and some of you are adulterers ! " —he turned to Sir Peter Wentworth, while he used an even stronger word when he addressed Henry Marten.

" Some of you are living in open contempt of God's commandments. Some of you are corrupt, unjust persons—how can you be a parliament for God's people ? Depart, I say, and let us have done with you. Go ! "

He stamped his foot and instantly the soldiers gathered round the shaking members.

Cromwell pointed to Sir Harry Vane. " One man might have prevented this," he went on, " but he is a juggler, and hath not so much as common honesty."

Vane and one or two others tried to remonstrate with the infuriated Cromwell, but, indicating the Speaker, he ordered : " Fetch him down ! "

The Speaker demurred ; whereupon Cromwell strode forward, and again cried to Harrison : " Take him down ! "

One of the most honourable men in that Parliament of apathy was young Algernon Sidney. It is a mystery why Cromwell should have singled him out for special attention.

Cromwell paused in his pacing and, standing in front of Sidney, roared, " Put *him* out ! "

Sidney stood upon his dignity and refused to leave, but when Harrison and another officer stepped forward and placed their hands significantly upon his shoulders he left the Chamber quietly.

Cromwell had not finished. Considerably put out himself, he was in a putting-out mood.

Looking round for something else upon which to vent his spleen, he caught sight of the mace. " Take away that bauble ! " he cried.

In a valorous attempt to restrain Cromwell from further exhibitions of temper, Alderman Allen remarked that if he would order the soldiers out of the Chamber an amicable settlement might be possible.

To which Cromwell retorted by calling Allen an

embezzler in relation to his office as Treasurer of the Army.

There was nothing for it but to leave the Chamber in as dignified a way as possible. Members began to file out, while Cromwell stood and glared.

As Sir Harry Vane passed the statuesque Oliver he called out, " This is not honest ; yea, it is against morality and common honesty."

Cromwell's voice was somewhat modified in tone as he replied : " Sir Harry Vane, Sir Harry Vane ! The Lord deliver me from Sir Harry Vane ! "

With the same abruptness that he had dealt with the members of the House of Commons he dissolved the Council of State.

Bradshaw, the President of the Council, was made of sterner stuff than the Speaker, and before taking his dismissal, he told Cromwell a few hard truths with as much sternness as he had displayed in Westminster Hall when Charles I was on trial.

Though Cromwell used strong language in describing some of the members of the Long Parliament, or the Rump Parliament as it was called, there is little wonder that he should lose his temper.

He believed in getting things done, but they were content to sit and achieve nothing. The Parliament had existed for such a time that members began to think they were there for life.

They challenged the power of the Army, and the leader of the Army himself. Many of them, no doubt, had the highest motives, but each had a different idea as to how the country should be governed.

The members might have remained in their seats for a considerable time longer had there not been a suggestion that they intended to form an alliance with the Presbyterians.

The word " Presbyterian " to Cromwell was like a red rag to a bull. As soon as he heard of the suggestion he began to talk about taking the Crown.

He consulted Whitelock, saying : " What if a man take upon him to be king ? "

The idea did not appeal to Whitelock, and he advised Cromwell not to pursue the matter. This weakness was the only instance of ambition for the Crown that Cromwell displayed, and it quickly passed.

Two months after the scene in the Commons he summoned by his own authority the Little, or Barebones', Parliament, named after Praise-God Barebones, a Fleet Street leather seller, who was one of the members.

Less than six months later the Barebones Parliament decided to resign its power into the hands of Cromwell who had, no doubt, previously arranged that it should do so.

On December 16, 1653, he became Lord Protector of the Commonwealth of England, Ireland, and Scotland.

In other hands such power might have developed into a tyranny.

XXV

KING CHARLES "THE MARTYR"

WHO was the mystery-executioner of Charles I ?
It is known that on the scaffold which stood
before the Banqueting House in Whitehall, there were
two masked men.

One was the common hangman ; the other, a stranger
who had never before been officially connected with an
execution. He, it is said, wielded the axe.

Years afterwards, particularly during the Restoration
period, attempts were made to fix the guilt on one or
other of the prominent Parliamentarians, without success.

The strongest evidence appears to have been that of
William Lily, the well-known astrologer, who was
examined before a parliamentary committee and testified :

> The next Sunday but one after Charles the First was
> beheaded, Robert Spavin, Secretary unto Lieutenant-general
> Cromwell, invited himself to dine with me, and brought Anthony
> Peirson, and several others along with him to dinner.
>
> Their principal discourse all dinner-time was only, who it
> was who beheaded the king. One said it was the common
> hangman ; another, Hugh Peters ; others were nominated,
> but none concluded.
>
> Robert Spavin, so soon as dinner was done, took me to the
> south window. Saith he : "These are all mistaken ; they
> have not named the man that did the fact : It was Lieutenant-
> colonel Joyce. I was in the room when he fitted himself for
> the work—stood behind him when he did it—when done went
> in again with him. There's no man knows this but my master
> [Cromwell], Commissary Ireton, and myself."
>
> "Doth not Mr Rushworth know it ?" saith I.

CHARLES THE FIRST
From a painting after Van Dyck
National Portrait Gallery

144

" No, he doth not," saith Spavin. The same thing Spavin since had often related to me when we were alone. Mr Prynne did, with much civility, make a report hereof to the house.

Charles II brought up the matter after the Restoration, and a certain William Hulett was charged with having beheaded the King. The following evidence was given in his defence :

> When my Lord Capell, Duke Hamilton, and the Earl of Holland, were beheaded in the Palace Yard, Westminster (soon after the king), my Lord Capell asked the common hangman, " Did you cut off my master's head ? "
>
> " Yes," saith he.
>
> " Where is the instrument that did it ? "
>
> He then brought the axe.
>
> " Is this the same axe ? " Lord Capell asked. " Are you sure ? "
>
> " Yes, my lord," saith the hangman. " I am very sure it is the same."
>
> My Lord Capell took the axe and kissed it, and gave him five pieces of gold. I heard him say, " Sirrah, wert thou not afraid ? "
>
> Saith the hangman, " They made me cut it off, and I had thirty pounds for my pains."

The theory has recently been propounded that the man who was beheaded was not Charles I at all. It is asserted that Charles employed a double to impersonate him on occasions when there was risk to his life.

Cromwell, it is said, was a party to the deception, and after the execution the King went to live in the West Country and was granted a pension by the Commonwealth Parliament in a fictitious name.

The last affecting scene between Charles and his family did more to influence later opinion towards the belief in the martyrdom of the King.

His young children came from Sion House to St James's Palace to bid him farewell. Taking the princess

10

in his arms, he kissed her and gave her two diamond seals, then prayed for a blessing upon the rest of his family, whereat " there was a great weeping."

Rising at daybreak, the King proceeded to dress himself with great care. " Death is not terrible to me," he said, " and, bless God, I am prepared."

Then an hour was spent with Bishop Juxon, and the King received the Sacrament.

" Now let the rogues come, I have heartily forgiven them, and am prepared for all I am to undergo."

At ten o'clock there was a rap at the door, and Colonel Hacker, pale as death, announced that everything was ready.

The solemn procession wended its way from St James's, through the park to Whitehall, passing the Horse Guards. The route was lined with soldiers, drums were beating, and colours flying.

The King did not shrink as he strode along between Colonel Tomlinson and Bishop Juxon, followed by his servants, bareheaded, and a guard of halberdiers.

Not a sound was heard from the crowds. Most of those people had clamoured for his execution, but now the grim reality had over-awed them.

At the scaffold they were not quite ready, so the King was led through the long gallery of the Banqueting House to his own Council Chamber. Food was laid before him, but he waved it aside, declaring that he would take nothing after the consecrated elements.

But about noon Bishop Juxon induced him to take a glass of claret and a piece of bread lest he " should be seized with faintness on the scaffold," and thus give the impression of cowardice.

The King walked out of the Banqueting House on to the scaffold " with the same unconcernedness and motion that he usually had when he entered it on a masque night," according to a witness who saw the execution from Wallingford House close by.

Expressions of sympathy now came from the crowd, and prayers were offered freely by both men and women. Even the soldiers standing around were affected by the scene.

Charles then began a speech to the crowds. He felt it his duty, he said, as an honest man, a good king, and a good Christian, to declare his innocence. He called God to witness that he never did begin a war upon the Parliament.

They had begun the war by claiming the militia. God would clear him, and being in charity with all, he would not lay this guilt upon the two Houses.

He added : " Ill instruments between me and the two Houses have been the chief cause of all this bloodshed. . . . Yet, for all this, God forbid I should be so ill a Christian as not to say that God's judgments are just upon me."

Alluding to the execution of Strafford, he continued : " An unjust sentence that I suffered to take effect is punished now by an unjust sentence on me."

He did not know, he said, who had been responsible for his death. " I do not desire to know ; I pray God forgive them."

Then he made an appeal on behalf of his son, and in his final remarks became inconsistent in declaring that the people ought never to have a share in the government—that being a thing " nothing pertaining to them," and calling himself " martyr of the people."

He concluded with a prayer that the people might take the right course for the benefit of the kingdom and their own salvation.

Having finished his speech, he turned to Colonel Hacker and said : " Take care that they do not put me to pain." To one of the masked executioners he observed : " I shall say but very short prayers, and thus thrust out my hands for the signal."

He put on his hat and asked, " Does my hair trouble you ? " The hair was tucked under his cap, and he said to Bishop Juxon, " I have good cause, and a gracious God on my side."

" You have now but one stage more," said Juxon. " The stage is turbulent and troublesome, but it is a short one ; it will soon carry you a very great way. It will carry you from earth to Heaven."

The last words of Charles were : " I go from a corruptible to an incorruptible crown, where no disturbance can be." And then the bishop responded : " You are exchanged from a temporal to an eternal crown—a good exchange."

The King took off his cloak, gave his locket, which contained the portrait of his wife Henrietta Maria, to Juxon, and with the word " Remember ! " stepped up to the block.

One blow from one of the masked figures ended his life. The other executioner, holding up the head, cried out : " This is the head of a traitor ! "

The body was embalmed and taken to Windsor to be interred. Parliament reluctantly allowed a few friends to conduct a funeral which was to cost no more than £500.

In the floor of the chapel a grave was already dug for the King, but, finding a vault in the centre of the choir containing two coffins believed to be those of Henry VIII and his Queen, Jane Seymour, they placed his coffin there.

There was no ceremony. The tears of the mourners fell silently upon the coffin of wood simply inscribed with the words, " King Charles " and the year of his death.

In the reign of William III the coffin was found when the vault was opened to take one of the children of Princess Anne, and remained forgotten for a century afterwards until the vault was reopened for another burial, and the lid of the coffin was raised.

The body of the King was found in good condition because of the gums and resins that had been used in embalming.

According to Sir Henry Halford :

> At length the whole face was disengaged from its covering. . . . The forehead and temples had lost little or nothing of their muscular substance . . . and the pointed beard, so characteristic of the reign of King Charles, was perfect. . . .

XXVI

George Fox, the Quaker of "Amiable Countenance"

"TREMBLE at the name of the Lord!" cried George Fox, the twenty-six-year-old shoemaker, when he faced Judge Gervase Bennett at Derby.

"Be quiet, you Quaker!" ordered the judge, and this name has stuck to the Society of Friends ever since.

William Penn saw nothing derogatory in the nickname. "'Tis much better," he said, "than Papist, Lutheran, or Calvinist, who are entirely ignorant of but enemies to quaking and trembling at the word of the Lord, as Moses and others did."

George Fox, with his sturdy frame and pious exhortations, was a remarkable personality. He was born in 1624 at Drayton-in-the-Clay, now called Fenny Drayton, in Leicestershire. His father was a weaver and was known as "Righteous Christer," while his mother was said to have belonged to the "stock of the martyrs."

As a youth he was employed by a shoemaker who also dealt in cattle and sheep. It would appear that much of his time was spent in looking after the sheep, for he was accustomed to use in his sermons metaphors connected with sheep.

One of his favourite sayings was : "Fear not the loss of the fleece, for it will grow again."

As Fox approached the state of manhood, he was obsessed by spiritual yearnings which the established churches could not satisfy.

GEORGE FOX 151

The rector of Fenny Drayton saw the lad's restlessness and shook his head with disapproval. He could offer no solace to a soul that was wandering, he believed, from the path of rectitude and orthodoxy.

Finally, Fox left his home and tramped the Midlands in search of spiritual guidance. The churches he visited made no appeal ; to him they were merely monuments of cold stone that savoured of medievalism.

He records in his diary how he wandered far and wide in his search, sometimes in "heavenly joy," and often in misery "great and heavy." Ultimately he reaches a stage when no man can help.

Then, suddenly, he is brought to "a first-hand knowledge of God," grounded upon his own conscience, for which he has to thank no outside authority.

In 1647, at the age of twenty-three, George Fox began his ministry in the Midlands. Two years later he received his first term of imprisonment for interrupting a sermon by declaring that the Holy Spirit was the only authority and guide.

In 1650 he appeared before Justice Gervase Bennett as a blasphemer and was committed to prison at Derby, but even at this early stage of his career he had won so much esteem that he was offered a captaincy in the Parliamentary Army, which he refused.

His constant persecution brought a wide response to his appeal, and before long he was joined by a number of other preachers.

The centre of the movement was at Swarthmore Hall, Ulverston, the home of Judge Fell, Cromwell's Chancellor of the Duchy of Lancaster, who was a patron of the Quakers, and whose wife, Margaret, became a member of the society.

Altogether he spent six years in various prisons, at Nottingham, Derby, Carlisle, London, Launceston,

Lancaster, Scarborough, and Worcester.   Frequently
he was confined under terrible conditions, but he
never retaliated.

During his ministry he wrote many pamphlets, which
were ungrammatical and full of mis-spellings.

Occasionally there appears a phrase which shows that
he had striking ability, and there is little doubt that he
was widely read.

Exposure and suffering made him a broken man by
the time he was forty, and after 1666 he spent most of his
time in an attempt to build up the connexion which had
been formed mainly through his efforts.

In 1669 he married Margaret, the widow of Judge
Fell, and then visited the West Indies and America,
Holland, and North Germany.   After his two years'
imprisonment in Worcester Gaol it took him a year to
recuperate.

His later years were passed chiefly in London, and
he was assisted by his wife.

Although his health finally broke down, he went about
London founding and organizing schools, and inter-
viewing members of Parliament to help in the framing of
the Toleration Act.

Fox was a strong opponent of ordinary church worship.
He called the churches " steeple-houses," and went
about nailing the following challenge upon the doors :

> God is not worshipped here : this is a temple made with
> hands : neither is this a church, for the church is in God.   This
> building is not in God, neither are you in Him, who meets here.

His violent antagonism to the clergy was strong to
the point of fanaticism.   His own *Journal* gives some
idea of how he regarded the Church :

> And I sat me down in the steeple-house till the priest had
> done : and he took a text, which was " Ho, every one that

thirsteth let him come freely without money and without price,
etc." And so I was moved to say unto him, " Come down, thou
deceiver, for dost thou bid people come freely and take of the
water of life freely : and yet thou takest £300 a year off them for
preaching the Scriptures to them ? Mayst thou not blush for
shame ? "

His rector at Fenny Drayton viewed Fox in a somewhat ironical light when he first began to preach, and
sarcastically remarked : " George Fox is come to the
light of the sun : and now he thinks to put out my
starlight."

Though persecuted by blows, stripes, stone-throwing,
and sometimes pistol-shots, he was always unmoved, and
often walked unarmed through a furious crowd.

Once when he was in prison he found among his
fellow-prisoners a young girl who was going to be hanged
for pilfering. He immediately sat down and wrote a
petition to the court, pointing out the absurdity of such
a punishment.

The court listened to his appeal, and the girl was
saved.

At the beginning of his wanderings his parents
were frequently called upon to stand surety for his
good behaviour. At last they began to fear, and
declared that he must take the entire responsibility
himself.

The first settled congregation of Friends was formed at
Mansfield, under the leadership of Fox, in 1648. Here
his first fellow-worker was Elizabeth Hooton, a woman
who came from Nottinghamshire.

Contemporary chroniclers describe his character in
a very favourable light. One writes : " He was a
goodly person and of amiable countenance." Another
declares that there were few men more abstemious
and temperate.

Though he never resisted a mob, his exceptional strength and endurance helped him to stand the buffeting which he received from time to time during his itinerant ministry.

If Fox was a fanatic in his desire to overthrow the established order of religion, it was a fanaticism less militant than that of some of the other reformers of the seventeenth century. It is said, too, that he possessed powers of healing, having cured his mother of a " dead palsy."

There is also record of the healing of a " distracted woman " at Skegby, Nottinghamshire.

Whether the stories of these cures are based on fact cannot be said with certainty, but there is no doubt that he was endowed with a psychic power that influenced his followers.

In his *Journal* he states that a man gave him a terrific blow with a stick on the back of his hand so that he " could not draw it in again." " But," he continues, " I looked at it in the love of God, and after a while the Lord's power sprang through me again, and through my hand and arm, so that in a moment I recovered strength in my hand and arm in the sight of them all."

Once an Ulverston mob attacked him and beat him senseless. He recovered to find himself " lying in a watery common, surrounded by people."

Fox seems to have made an impression on the inflexible temperament of Oliver Cromwell, for when the Protector was offered the Crown, Fox was one of those who advised him strongly against acceptance. It is believed that the Quaker's pleadings were among those which had the most weight.

Fox had a sarcastic vein which he could exercise when he felt inclined. The excessive politeness of society

annoyed him because of its insincerity.   Thus, he writes
of this social effusion :

> " How do you do, sir ? " doff the hat, scrape a leg, make a
> curtsey.   " I am glad to see you well," " Your servant," " your
> servant, my lord (or sir) or mistress " ;   and when they are past
> them, with the same tongue wish evil to them, speak evil of
> them, and laugh at one another behind their backs.

George Fox died at the house of Henry Gouldney, in
White Hart Court, Gracechurch Street, where he had
preached only a few days previously.

XXVII

Louis XIV, King for Seventy-two Years

MADAME DE MAINTENON, a mistress whom Louis XIV made a wife and virtually a queen, appears to have shown little emotion either during his illness or at his death-bed.

"I have always heard that it is a difficult thing to die," Louis said to her three days before his death. "I am now on the verge of this predicament, and I do not find the process of dissolution so painful a one."

She replied that it was a terrible moment if one still cherished an attachment to the world and had restitutions to make.

To this the King responded, "As an individual I owe restitution to no one; and as regards what I owe the kingdom I trust in the mercy of God. I have duly confessed myself; my confessor declares that I have a great reliance in God; I have it with all my heart."

On the following day he said to Madame de Maintenon, "What consoles me in quitting you is the hope that we shall soon be united in eternity."

She made no reply, but on quitting the chamber she was heard to remark, "See the appointment which he makes with me! This man has never loved anyone but himself."

She thereupon left for her home at Saint Cyr.

When the King's illness took a change for the worse, the ladies and gentlemen of the Court concerned themselves more with the Duke of Orleans, the future Regent.

But when the King rallied they returned to his bed-chamber and left the Duke alone.

And so it went on.

Then the King noticed the absence of Madame de Maintenon.

He was annoyed. He asked that she appear immediately.

She returned, gave an excuse for her absence, and throughout the following day remained by the King's bedside.

Towards evening it was clear that a few hours would see the end.

Madame de Maintenon returned to her room, divided the furniture among the servants, and left for Saint Cyr. She was never seen at the King's bedside again.

No tears were shed when the King died. The country was relieved because he had ruled autocratically ; Europe was glad, for he had been a constant menace.

He had reigned over France for seventy-two years and had made many conquests. It was not until the last fifteen years of his life that his war-like propensities had been subdued.

Born on September 16, 1638, Louis succeeded to the throne of France at the age of four.

For the first ten years his hold upon the crown was precarious. During the civil war of the Fronde, the young King, his mother, and Cardinal Mazarin wandered about the country in search of refuge.

In 1653 the civil war came to an end, and in the next year Louis began his first campaign in Flanders against the Spaniards. In 1655 Spain was humiliated.

When Ferdinand, Emperor of Rome, died in 1657, every possible scheme was put in hand to make Louis his successor. But Leopold of Austria was appointed instead.

By a treaty of peace with Spain it was stipulated that Louis should marry the Infanta Maria Theresa, daughter of Philip IV. The marriage was celebrated with great magnificence in 1666.

The young queen brought with her a dowry of half a million crowns, but she was intellectually weak and childish. Louis treated her with respect, but there never was much love between them.

Mazarin died in March, 1661, and Louis immediately took over all the reins of government.

" To whom shall we address ourselves on affairs of State ? " said the courtiers of Louis.

" To me, of course," he replied, to their amazement.

And it was this attitude that he maintained to the end of his reign—" *L'état, c'est moi.*"

" I claim," he said, " the full and entire disposal of all property, whether in the possession of clergy or of laymen."

Parliament was rendered ineffective. He ordered members to cease discussing his edicts and to register them instead.

He broke the spirit of the nobles, subdued the clergy, and treated the common people as if they were dogs.

His ambition and arrogance soon caused trouble between France and her neighbours. He insulted the Pope, and treated the Protestants harshly.

On the death of his father-in-law, Philip IV, who was succeeded by an infant son, he seized the opportunity to invade the Low Countries, then in the occupation of Spain.

A large part of the country had been conquered by his 50,000 men before the Spanish Council at Brussels was aware the invasion had begun.

At last the unscrupulous ambition of Louis caused a triple alliance between England, Sweden, and Holland,

and Louis was forced to sign the treaty of Aix-la-Chapelle in 1668.

Louis then turned against the Dutch, and Amsterdam was only saved by flooding the surrounding country.

Other continental nations made common cause against Louis, and after the war had lasted nearly seven years it terminated in 1678 with the Treaty of Nimeguen, which left France in possession of important towns in Spanish Flanders.

In 1682 he seized the Papal town of Anjou.

Next year he sent an expedition against Algiers and reduced it with Tunis and Tripoli. The Genoese, who had supplied powder to Algiers, had to send an ambassador to Paris to apologize.

In 1683-4, Louis took possession of towns on the Rhine, Dixmude, and Courtrai, and bombarded Luxembourg.

Louis, now at the height of his power, called himself God's vicegerent on earth.

To receive the adulation of the people he made a royal progress through his dominions with two of his mistresses, De La Vallière and Madame de Montespan, in the State carriage with him and his wife.

The Queen died in 1683, and within two years Louis married Madame de Maintenon.

During the remaining thirty years of his reign this woman exercised a great influence over him and tried to restrain his ambitions.

Louis had much power in Europe. England was easy to handle during the reign of Charles II owing to the large bribes which Louis planted in England.

When the expedition of the Prince of Orange was on the way to depose James II, Louis offered his assistance to the Stuart. French troops were used by James at the battle of the Boyne.

For the next ten years Louis was continuously at war against a European confederation.

War was proclaimed against him at Vienna on May 15, 1702, and eventually his armies were beaten by the Duke of Marlborough and Prince Eugene.

It ended in the Treaty of Utrecht.

Two years later Louis died.

XXVIII

Sir Isaac Newton, Sickly Child and Famous Scientist

WHEN Isaac Newton was born he was such a sickly child that " he might have been put into a quart jug," but his physique was normal within a few years.

He was born on Christmas Day, 1642 (old style), the year in which Galileo, another famous astronomer, died.

Newton's father had died before his birth, and when he was three years old his mother was married a second time—to the Rev. Barnabas Smith.

Isaac was sent to small day-schools at Skillington and Stoke, in Lincolnshire, and at the age of twelve went to a public school at Grantham.

He did badly at first because of an inferiority complex, and because of the persecution of one of the other boys, who was a bully and the acknowledged head of the school.

Newton determined to be revenged.

He first of all challenged the boy to a fight and, having trounced him soundly, strove successfully to surpass him in learning.

He became head of the school, and during his leisure hours made all kinds of mechanical appliances. He built windmills, water-clocks, sundials, and a carriage which could be driven by the person who sat upon it.

One of his pastimes was kite-flying. He made kites of such peculiar shapes that he attracted a good deal of attention in Lincoln.

One kite which he flew at night with a lantern on the tail caused consternation around the countryside. The local people saw the light swinging in the sky and thought it was a meteor of eccentric tendencies.

Newton was also a good artist. He copied portraits and wrote verses.

On the death of his stepfather in 1656, young Isaac was taken from school to help in the management of his mother's little farm.

Although he carried out his duties satisfactorily and attended the local markets, he was more interested in science, and his books were more attractive than buying and selling farm-produce.

At last his distaste for a farmer's life caused him to be sent back to school at Grantham, where he remained for nine months preparing for a university course.

He went to Cambridge in June, 1661, and was admitted to Trinity College.

He bought a book on astrology which contained such puzzling diagrams that he had recourse to Euclid to assist him in understanding them. Later, he threw Euclid aside as " a trifling book," and turned to Descartes' *Geometry*.

In the summer of 1665 he had to leave Cambridge because of the plague. It is believed that it was during this year that he began to study the question of the force of gravity, and to speculate upon the problem that the same force which brought an apple to the ground governed the moon and the planets and kept them in their orbits.

In 1666 he obtained a glass prism and experimented " to try therewith the phenomena of colours." A year later he was elected a minor fellow at Cambridge, and took his M.A., being twenty-third on the list of 148.

SIR ISAAC NEWTON
Engraved from the portrait by Kneller

162

A temporary reappearance of the plague stopped his studies for a time, but at the end of 1668 he made a reflecting telescope over six inches long with a magnifying power of thirty-eight, which showed him Jupiter's four moons and the crescent of Venus.

Next year he was appointed Lucasian professor of mathematics, and from this time began to communicate with the Royal Society, for his discoveries had already created much interest in the scientific world.

His reflecting telescope was sent to the society and inspected by the King. Before the end of the year a Fellow of Trinity College had constructed an instrument which Newton acknowledged was better than his own.

Newton was elected a Fellow of the Royal Society on January 10, 1671, and a week afterwards he offered to read an account of what, in his judgment, " was the oddest, if not the most considerable detection which had hitherto been made in the operation of Nature."

This was his discovery that white light consisted of rays of different colours and different refrangibility ; but it was not allowed to go unchallenged.

Hook, Huygens, and several other ' inferior people ' so upset his tranquillity that he said he would be no longer " a slave to philosophy," but would give it up altogether, except for his own satisfaction.

He began to find mathematical theories dry, and decided to apply for the law-fellowship. When some one else was appointed to the post Newton asked the Royal Society to excuse him from its weekly payments.

In December, 1675, Newton communicated another discovery to the Royal Society. It was a " theory of light and colours." Hook, after he had read it, declared that most of it was already contained in his *Micrographia*. Whereupon there was a controversy between Newton and Hook, which lasted for some time.

Later there was a controversy on certain principles given in Newton's *Principia*. The doctrines put forward were said to have been discovered by Leibnitz, and for two centuries there was a cleavage of opinion as to who had the prior right of discovery.

Sir David Brewster in his *Life of Newton* claims that Newton should have the credit for the invention of the method of fluxions in 1666, although the principle of it was not published to the world until 1687.

Newton was one of the deputation which protested against the granting to a monk of the degree of Master of Arts. They appeared before the notorious Judge Jeffreys, who rebuked them and remarked : " As most of you are divines, go away and sin no more lest a worse thing come unto you."

Sir David Brewster records that

> Under this rebuke, and in front of such a judge, the most ferocious that ever sat upon the judgment seat, stood the immortal author of the *Principia*, who had risen from the invention of its problems to defend the religion which he professed and the university which he adored.
>
> The mandate which he resisted—a diploma to a monk—was in one sense an abuse of trivial magnitude, unworthy of the intellectual sacrifice which it occasioned ; but the spark is no measure of the conflagration which it kindles, and the arm of a Titan may be required to crush what the touch of an infant might have destroyed.

Newton's efforts in connexion with this protest were rewarded after the revolution by his being chosen in 1689 to sit in Parliament for the University, but when it was dissolved in 1690 he failed to obtain re-election.

His friends tried to obtain for him the Presidency of King's College, Cambridge, but in vain. Another attempt to get him appointed to the mastership of the Charterhouse School was also unsuccessful,

In the autumn of 1692 his health began to give way. For nearly a year he could not sleep. He lost his appetite, and suffered with neurasthenia to such an extent that he was reported to be insane.

This belief prevailed for years and was never really eradicated, but as he wrote during this period his four celebrated letters to Dr Bentley and was carrying on researches of a chemical nature, there can be little truth in the story of his insanity.

Despite the discoveries which Newton had made, there seemed little inclination on the part of the Government to reward him, until his friend, Charles Montague, whom he had known as a Fellow of Trinity, was appointed Chancellor of the Exchequer.

He appointed Newton in 1696 Warden of the Mint at a salary of £600 a year. Three years later he became master of this establishment with a salary of £1200 a year.

In the same year the French Academy elected him one of their eight foreign associates.

In 1703 Newton was elected President of the Royal Society. He advocated the publication of the observations made at Greenwich Observatory, and approached the Prince Consort on the point, who offered to pay the cost.

Articles of agreement were drawn up, whereby Flamsteed, who was responsible for the observations, agreed to supply them. In the end he failed to fulfil his contract ; a quarrel followed, and Flamsteed declared that Newton was his enemy.

Newton is said to have acted unjustly in the matter, and to have given way to " sudden ebullitions of temper " and " apparent perversity of conduct."

Despite this controversy, Newton was knighted on April 16, 1705, when the Queen, with the Prince Consort, was passing through Cambridge to her residence at Newmarket.

The Court was held at Trinity Lodge, and the celebrations were so extensive that the University had to borrow £500 to pay the cost.

On the accession of George I, Charles Montague was made Earl of Halifax and appointed First Lord of the Treasury. Through his friendship with Newton he became acquainted with Newton's niece, Catherine Barton, a woman of considerable beauty.

He admired her so much that he left her the rangership and lodge of Bushey Park, with £5000 and an annuity of £200, purchased in Newton's name.

This legacy was viewed with suspicion by many people, and Newton did not escape being involved in the suggestion that he had contrived the whole thing.

Sir Isaac Newton was a great favourite at the Court of George I, and to undermine his reputation, Leibnitz, the German philosopher, charged Newton with certain offences. When the King heard of it, Newton had to defend himself.

Five papers were submitted by Leibnitz, but the trouble was ended by the death of the German philosopher himself.

Newton was eighty when he was attacked with illness, and lingered on for some time. The fatigue of presiding at the meeting of the Royal Society in March 2, 1727, was the beginning of the end.

On March 18 he became insensible, and he died at Kensington on the morning of March 20, 1727, in his eighty-fifth year.

His body, taken to London, lay in state in the Jerusalem Chamber. It was then taken to Westminster Abbey and buried near the entrance of the choir, where a monument was erected by his relatives.

XXIX

The Rise and Fall of the Duke of Marlborough

IT is inconceivable that the defection of one mistress should have caused much concern to Charles II. He was, however, intensely annoyed when he found that John Churchill was having an affair with the celebrated Barbara Villiers, Duchess of Cleveland.

The Duke of Buckingham, who never lost an opportunity of keeping in the King's good graces, whether it involved the disgrace of another or not, told the King what was going on.

Churchill had to jump out of a window.

The Duchess was so fond of Churchill that to console him she gave him £5000. With due regard to the value of money—his family was poor—young John invested this sum in the purchase of an annuity.

Churchill married Sarah Jennings, a woman of no great means, but possessed of wit, beauty, and an unusually forceful character.

From the date of this marriage Churchill's fortunes began. He might have been even more powerful but for the fact that during his career he had a tendency to wobble from a cause and thus support first one side and then the other.

Churchill was born at Ashe in Devonshire on May 26, 1650. His father, Sir Winston Churchill, was a loyal supporter of the Stuarts, for which he was rewarded with places at Court for two of his children.

Sir Winston's daughter, Arabella, became maid of

honour to the Duchess of York, and his son, John, page to the Duke. The Duke of York, afterwards James II, soon put Arabella on the list of his mistresses, and John lost no opportunity of making capital out of the fact.

At the age of eighteen the Duke made him an ensign in the Guards, and he fought at Tangier, an English possession besieged by the Moors.

On his return home occurred the affair with the Duchess of Cleveland, and his ignominious flight from the presence of the King.

Charles apparently bore no malice, for in 1672 John went with his regiment to Holland and fought against the Dutch under the Duke of Monmouth, and distinguished himself in his twenty-third year as captain of grenadiers. His bravery was admired by Monmouth, and he was publicly thanked by Louis XIV and specially recommended to the King's favour.

The King of France made him colonel of an English regiment which was at that time under Louis's command. In 1676 John returned to England to find himself in great favour and confidence of his sister's lover, the Duke of York.

He married Sarah Jennings in 1678.

She ruled him with discretion and kept him away from the temptations of Court.

He was now in charge of a regiment of infantry.

When James succeeded to the throne in 1685 Churchill went to Paris to inform the French monarch of the fact, and to thank him for a gift of money which James had badly needed.

On his return he was made Baron Churchill of Sandridge in Hertfordshire.

When overtures for the Crown were made by William of Orange, Churchill was the medium of correspondence between him and Princess Anne. At the same time he was preparing the English for the proposed change of government.

James was on the way with his army to meet the Prince of Orange before he suspected any treachery, for he had recently raised Churchill to the rank of Lieutenant-general.

At a council of war on the evening of November 23, 1688, Churchill saw that he was suspected, and in the night he fled to the Prince's quarters, together with the Duke of Grafton.

This defection proved the undoing of James, who retreated to London to find that his daughter, Anne, had left the palace with Lady Churchill.

James refused to make concessions to the people or to forgive those who had revolted. " I cannot do it," he exclaimed. " I must make examples ; Churchill above all—Churchill whom I raised so high. He and he alone has done this. He has corrupted my army. He has corrupted my child. He would have put me into their hands, but for God's special providence."

On the accession of William, however, he was appointed a lord of the bedchamber, and created Earl of Marlborough. In 1689 he was sent to command the English forces fighting the French in Holland.

Back in London, Marlborough got into touch with the Jacobites, but they saw through his plan to place Anne on the throne, and govern in her name.

On January 9, 1692, Anne and Queen Mary had a dispute, as Marlborough's activities had become known. Next morning he was dismissed from all his offices and forbidden to appear at Court.

The Earl was thrown into the Tower through a forged Jacobite document which contained his name, but when the forgery was discovered he was released on bail, his name being struck out of the list of privy councillors.

Later he was restored to the Council and appointed to command the forces in the Netherlands.

When William died and Anne succeeded, Marlborough immediately received the Garter, was made Commander-in-Chief, and was placed in full command of the army in the war with the French.

The conduct of the campaign between 1704 and 1711 is well known. Though he suffered from dim sight, headache, fever, and ague he accomplished some of the greatest military exploits in the history of England.

In 1702 he was made Duke of Marlborough.

Despite these great achievements there were movements at home to bring about his downfall. The Duchess, too, had become more grasping, and though the Queen gave in to her demands for a while, she at last refused to submit to dictation.

A break between the two women occurred in April 1710. Marlborough suffered continual insult from the court, and at last was deprived of his offices.

Charges of peculation were laid against him, and the former charges of treason renewed.

The situation was so painful that Marlborough had no alternative but to escape to the Continent.

One day a packet-boat left Dover with the Duke aboard. He travelled as an ordinary private passenger.

If England did not want this great military hero, the feelings of Belgium were otherwise. As soon as the townspeople of Ostend heard that the famous Duke of Marlborough was on board the boat they fired a salute of all their cannon.

People crowded round him, shook his hands, and tears came into their eyes when they thought of the ingratitude of England.

Even a Frenchman cried : " Though this sight is worth a million to my king, yet, I believe, he would not, at such a price, have lost the service of so brave a man."

When Queen Anne died, Marlborough considered it safe to return to England. He landed at Dover on August 1, 1714, the day on which George I was proclaimed.

What a contrast to his departure ! The cannon roared, and hundreds of people stood on the sea front to cheer him. All the way to London his progress was a triumphant one.

At Southwark he was met by a large company of City dignitaries, who escorted him into the one square mile.

He proceeded to St James's with the crowd displaying more enthusiasm for his return than for the accession of George I.

They cried, " Long live the King ! " but it was a mightier shout that echoed, " Long live the Duke of Marlborough ! "

For two years Marlborough enjoyed the favour of the Hanoverian Court. The undemonstrative George I was heard to remark, " Marlborough's retirement would give me as much pain as if a dagger should be plunged into my bosom."

Even so, Marlborough was not free from attacks. It is said that during the 1715 rebellion, he lent money to the Jacobites, at the same time advising the Government how to suppress the rebels.

This seems hardly credible, for at the time Marlborough's health was beginning to fail. Old age was creeping on, and in 1716 he retired to his country-seat at Blenheim.

His life ebbed slowly over a period of six years, and with recurring attacks of paralysis he became completely helpless some time before he died on June 16, 1722.

The Duke was seventy-two at his death. With national honours the remains were buried in Westminster Abbey.

It is hard to believe that a warlike man such as Marlborough should always have yearned for peace.

A paragraph in a letter which he wrote home at the time of the siege of Douay, however, might well serve as a precept for the nations of to-day :

> It is impossible, without seeing it, to be sensible of the misery of this country. At least one-half of the people of the villages, since the beginning of last winter, are dead, and the rest look as if they came out of their graves. It is so mortifying that no Christian can see it but must, with all his heart, wish for a speedy peace.

XXX

PETER, GREATEST OF ALL THE TSARS

PETER THE GREAT was a quick-change artist.
One day he would be a plain " Mister," the next
he would observe all the conventions of kingship.

He was one of the most extraordinary men who ever
strode the stage of history. He was full of contradictions,
but when his acts are reviewed in a logical light, there is
nothing to suggest that he was inconsistent.

Voltaire writes :

> He gave a polish to his people, and was himself a savage ;
> he taught them the art of war, of which he was himself ignorant ;
> from the sight of a small boat on the river Moskwa he erected a
> powerful fleet, made himself an expert and active shipwright,
> sailor, pilot, and commander ; he changed the manners,
> customs, and laws of the Russians, and lives in their memory
> as the father of his country.

He had a passion for ships and navigation and, as a
young man, a mania for remaking Russia on the basis
of Western civilization. He resolved upon a tour of
Western Europe and started with Holland. There in
the dockyard of Saardam, he took off his coat and worked
as a dockyard labourer. Adopting the name of Peter
Michaeloff, he drew his wages with the rest, got up early
in the morning, and cooked his own breakfast.

Having acquired all there was to know of the manual
side of shipbuilding, he came to England in January, 1698,
to study the theory of the art. He dropped his guise of
workman for that of a private gentleman, and three ships

having been sent to bring him and his companions to this country, he declared that he wished to remain incognito.

But King William insisted that he should live in royal splendour, and although his name was never mentioned as king, he was allotted a large house and suite in Buckingham Street, Adelphi. He was placed in charge of the Marquess of Carmarthen, and the two became firm friends, and used to spend their evenings together, drinking hot brandy spiced with pepper.

It is said that Peter the Great was fond of strong liquor, and was particularly partial to a potion called nectar ambrosia, which had recently been introduced and had taken the fancy of the King.

The Tsar remained in England for four months. Contemporary records give some idea of his movements : one day visiting Kensington Palace, another going to the Opera or to the Temple revels, yet another to Woolwich and Deptford to see the dockyards. He was fond of theatres and dances, and was often present at social functions, but always as a private gentleman.

He also went to Redriff, where he was having a ship built, and was present at the launch of a battleship at Chatham.

Peter detested the streets of London, with their jostling and hurrying crowds. Amsterdam had been bad enough, but London was worse, and he frequently lost his patience.

Once he was walking along the Strand with the Marquess of Carmarthen when he was jostled by a porter carrying a load on his shoulder. The Tsar was rudely pushed into the road, whereat he was much indignant and walked up to the man intending to strike him. A serious *contretemps* would have occurred but for the Marquess, who pulled the Tsar back, explaining to the porter who he was.

PETER THE GREAT

The porter was amused. Turning round with a grin, he said : " Tsar ! We are all Tsars here ! "

After having lived a month in London the Tsar moved to Deptford to a house recently in the occupation of Admiral Benbow. A hole was made through the wall between the residence and the dockyard so that the Tsar could enter the dockyard when he chose without attracting the attention of outsiders.

A beautiful garden was laid out in the grounds of the house. A good deal of money was spent in the work, as Admiral Benbow had not been quite so careful in preserving the garden as he might have been ; but the Tsar was an even worse tenant.

The servant of John Evelyn, the landlord of the house, wrote to his master giving a very indifferent character to the tenants. He said :

> There is a house full of people right nasty. The Tsar lies next your library, and dines in the parlour next your study. He dines at ten o'clock and six at night ; is very often at home a whole day ; very often in the King's yard, or by water, dressed in several dresses. The King is expected there this day ; the best parlour is pretty clean for him to be entertained in. The King pays for all he has.

The shortcomings of Peter the Great did not end there. It is said that he pushed a wheelbarrow through a favourite holly-hedge of Evelyn's merely for exercise. Although the Tsar and his servants remained at the house only three weeks, they did £150 worth of damage, which was a considerable sum in the seventeenth century.

Peter seems to have been an adept at picking up information, for in the short time he spent at Deptford he learned enough to alter the masts, rigging, and sails of the *Royal Transport*, a ship which William had presented to him. Day after day he could be seen on the Thames in a sailing yacht or rowing a boat alone. Sometimes he would take members of his suite for a trip in a boat, the suite rowing and he himself steering.

What the members of his suite thought of this procedure is not recorded, but as he succeeded in getting them to believe that they would receive command of ships when they reached home no doubt they were happy.

Then, when the party had finished their day's outing, the Tsar and his followers would call at a public-house in Great Tower Street, smoke their pipes, and drink beer and brandy.

The landlord of the inn was an opportunist. Very soon there appeared above the front door the Tsar of Muscovy's head. The sign remained until the beginning of the nineteenth century, when a collector of inn-signs obtained it from the then landlord and put a new one in its place.

In the eyes of Peter, Greenwich Hospital was a palatial building, much too elaborate as a home for old pensioned seamen. One day the King asked him how he liked the hospital, and the Tsar replied, " If I were the adviser of your Majesty, I should counsel you to remove your court to Greenwich, and convert St James's into a hospital."

During the law term, Peter paid a visit to Westminster Hall, where he was struck by the advocates, wearing gowns and wigs, appearing always in a hurry.

" Who are these people ? " he inquired.

" They are lawyers," was the reply.

" Lawyers ! " cried the Tsar in astonishment, " why, I have but two in the whole of my dominions, and I believe I shall hang one of them the moment I get home."

In the Bodleian Library at Oxford there is a landlord's bill relating to an hotel at Godalming, where Peter the Great stayed following a review of the fleet.

There were twenty-one in the party, and the bill of costs indicates either the cupidity of the landlord, or the amazing capacity of the Tsar and his suite for disposing of food and drink.

At breakfast the party consumed half a sheep, a quarter of lamb, ten pullets, twelve chickens, three quarts of brandy, six quarts of mulled wine, seven dozen of eggs with salad. At dinner they disposed of five ribs of beef, weighing three stone, one sheep weighing 56 lb., three-quarters of a lamb, a boiled shoulder and loin of veal, eight pullets, eight rabbits, two dozen and a half of sack, and one dozen claret.

Peter's liquor-consumption was tremendous. He is known to have drunk a pint of brandy and a bottle of sherry as an appetizer during the morning, while in the evening eight bottles of sack were easily disposed of ; and after that he would go to the theatre.

The Tsar was over-awed by Parliament. He attended debates, but only on the roof of the House, where he could look through a little window and see what was going on. At last the King laughed at him for his timidity, and he gave up spying upon Parliament in this undignified manner.

One of Peter's favourite occupations was taking watches to pieces.

When he left England he took with him about 500 artificers of all trades, including captains of ships, sail-makers, pilots, gunners, surgeons, compass-makers, carvers, and coppersmiths. Calling upon King William just before his departure, he handed to him a ruby valued at £10,000 which he had brought in his waistcoat pocket wrapped up in a small piece of brown paper.

Peter the First of Russia was born at Moscow on May 30, 1672. In Europe he got practically what he wanted. He formed an army disciplined on European

12

tactics aided by a Scotsman, Patrick Gordon, and he appropriated land here and there. From Sweden he took a portion of Ingria, where he laid the foundations of St Petersburg. Then followed a long contest with the Swedes in which Peter was generally worsted, but in the end he had his revenge when he routed the Swedish king at Poltava in 1709.

In 1712 he married Catherine, and in 1716 the two made a tour of Europe. About this time he ordered the execution of his son Alexei. He died in the arms of his wife on January 28, 1725.

XXXI

Voltaire, Precursor of the French Revolution

VOLTAIRE was among the most misunderstood men in history. Because of his unremittirg attacks on Christianity an impression has been left in the lay mind of a sinister figure actuated by some devilish influence.

That he did try to cast doubt upon the Scriptures goes without saying. "Write what you will," said an opponent on one occasion, "you will not destroy the Christian religion."

"We shall see about that," was Voltaire's reply. This was not the boast of an egotistic man ; he believed he could do as he said.

Where Voltaire erred was in thinking that the falseness of the religion of his day was typical of Christianity as exemplified by the superstition, hypocrisy, and intolerance that ruled everywhere, disgracing the French nation, its Government, and Court.

He was not a revolutionary, but his theories did much to provoke the Revolution, for, in exposing the condition of the Romish Church of his day, and modelling the French mind to his own unbelief, he paved the way unconsciously for the atrocities and blasphemies of the Revolution.

Voltaire began life as François Marie Arouet. The " de Voltaire " was assumed by him in after life, on his being left the family property.

His father, Francois Arouet, was treasurer of local

revenues, and his mother, Margaret Aumart, belonged to a noble family of Poitou.

Because of the feeble constitution of the infant, the baptismal rites were not performed for months after his birth. His father, a man of means, was able to give his second son a liberal education, and although not an eminent scholar, he assimilated enough knowledge for his literary work.

He was instructed by tutors in a Jesuit college, and it was here that his first heretical tendencies began to show themselves.

One of the masters, it is said, predicted that the boy would become an advocate of deism as opposed to the doctrines of the Church, and when a friend of the family, Abbé Châteauneuf, in common with other well-known pillars of the Church, deliberately avowed his own unbelief, the seeds thus sown in the mind of Arouet grew into a strenuous opposition to orthodoxy.

He was to be found in the salons of Paris, where his literary aptitude and advanced opinions made him welcome. Already many were indignant at the hypocrisy and licence which prevailed at the court of Versailles, and were working for the removal of all religious beliefs.

But Voltaire did not go to the lengths of some who were professed atheists ; he took his stand upon deism, and it was as a deist that he attacked the revelation of the Gospels.

The fascinations of Paris were dangerous for the youth, and his father hastened to remove him from temptation by obtaining for him an appointment in the suite of the Marquis of Châteauneuf, the French Ambassador at The Hague.

Having a flirtatious tendency, young Arouet soon

became entangled with a woman. This caused his speedy return to Paris.

It was about this time that he conceived the ideas for two of his most noted works, the *Henriade* and the *Age of Louis XIV*. Louis had lately died, disgraced in the eyes of the people.

Soon after the King's death several pamphlets of a satirical nature insulting to his memory were published. Arouet, who had already become widely known as a wit, was accused of being the author of some of them.

Merely on suspicion he was committed to the Bastille, where he did much writing. His release was obtained by the Duc d'Orléans, and at the age of twenty-four Voltaire's tragedy, *Œdipe*, was produced.

It was this play which embittered him against society, for before it could be performed in Paris, he had to submit to its being altered to suit the prevailing taste, thus embodying principles to which he could not honestly subscribe.

He became the object of malice on the part of his rivals, and when his second play was a failure they were overjoyed.

In 1722 Voltaire visited Holland and called upon Rousseau. A short friendship ended in jealousy and an antipathy on the part of Rousseau which lasted for years.

Two years later appeared the first French epic poem, *Henriade*. It was first printed in a corrected form in London, and was dedicated to Caroline, the wife of George II.

Soon afterwards Voltaire was again in the Bastille for some vague offence, and at the end of six months' imprisonment he was ordered to leave Paris.

He came to England, and soon expressed his admiration of the civil and religious liberties of this country.

He became acquainted with many of the leading English writers, and was particularly drawn towards Newton, Bolingbroke, Pope, and others.

Here Voltaire was free to take his stand for the principles of deism, despite the ridicule of the atheists. During his stay in England he wrote the tragedy of *Brutus* and another tragedy which was never performed.

Having private means, Voltaire was not subject to the whims and fancies of rich benefactors, and could propagate his beliefs with independence. The theatre, however, was the only safe method of doing this, and he used it at every opportunity.

The play *Zaïre* he composed in little more than a fortnight. It was a success; but he also met with failures.

While in England he collected material for his life of Charles XII of Sweden, and also for his *Lettres sur les Anglais*, which, published at a later date, gave the French an idea of the liberty of conscience enjoyed by Englishmen as compared with the conditions in France.

La Pucelle was a piece which sent Voltaire's opponents frantic. Before it was published his enemies learned the theme and declared that it was an offence against morality.

It was in connexion with the criticism of this work that Voltaire declared that he would kill Christianity.

Discussing the way in which people were sent to the Bastille for little or no offence on false commitment orders, Voltaire once asked : " What do you do with those who forge *lettres de cachet* ? "

" Oh, we hang them," was the reply.

" That is well so far," said Voltaire, " until we come to the time when we hang those who write the *genuine lettres de cachet*."

Which indicates the extent of Voltaire's prejudice against officialdom.

By this time Voltaire was beginning to realize that his enemies were determined to get rid of him by fair means or foul.

He was continually persecuted, so that his work was beginning to suffer, and finding a kindred spirit in the Marchioness du Châtelet, a learned woman and a philosopher, he decided to go with her to a retreat that would be less irksome.

In a quiet spot on the borders of Champagne and Lorraine Voltaire wrote an exposition of the discoveries of Newton in astronomy and optics, but he could not obtain permission for the publication of the book.

He then produced among other works his history of Charles XII of Sweden, and made preparation for his history of Louis XIV, and the essay on the manners and spirit of nations.

While at Cirey, too, he began a correspondence with Frederick the Great of Prussia, who was himself ambitious in the literary field, and was particularly anxious for fame as a writer of French.

Asked to criticize some of Frederick's work, it is to be feared that Voltaire gave a too glowing account of the MS. This led to a friendship which was often prejudiced by egotism on both sides.

In 1746 he was admitted a member of the French Academy. About this time he lost his collaborator, the Marchioness, and following this misfortune he returned to Paris, and resumed his labours, producing the plays *Semiramis*, *Orestes*, and *Rome Sauvée*.

Having to put up with the persecution of his literary rivals, he accepted again the proffered friendship of Frederick the Great and went to Berlin, where they became boon companions.

But two men of the same vain temperament could not agree for long. There was mutual disgust, suspicion, and even hatred, and Voltaire had to leave Berlin in a hurry, with Frederick doing his best to prevent his escape.

Paris would not have him, so he was compelled to live at Ferney with his niece, Mme Denis, a widow without children.

Many of his noted writings were composed at his Ferney retreat. In 1757 he edited an edition of his complete works, but continued to vent his dislike of Christianity, in which he was completely unrestrained, and often descended to the worst vituperation, all of which made a lasting impression upon French democracy, and earned the enmity of the aristocracy and the Church.

The theatrical circle of Paris was always his friend, and with this support he ignored his literary rivals who had coalesced with Jesuits and profligate courtiers to attack him.

He returned to Paris, and there he received so great a reception from the theatres that he was induced to declare : " I shall be suffocated under the weight of these offerings."

But the excitement and exertions began to tell upon him, and he died on May 30, 1778, in his eighty-fourth year.

XXXII

John Wesley's Virago-wife

WHEN John Wesley, in his forty-eighth year, married Mrs Vizelle, a widow with four children and a respectable income, he stipulated that he should be allowed to preach as many sermons as usual, and travel just as many miles.

As Wesley had some time before published *Thoughts on a Single Life*, in which he had exhorted those who were single to remain so, this arrangement no doubt satisfied his own conscience and the qualms of his followers.

But Mrs Wesley, while prepared to take John on those terms, found married life somewhat irksome.

At first she resolutely lived the life and travelled with Wesley, but it was too hazardous, particularly as he would not take any of her money. Nor did she feel very comfortable in the company of the humble Methodists.

She began to feel sorry for herself and then to complain, but her husband was too full of his work to take her grumblings seriously.

From discontent to jealousy is a short step, and Mrs Wesley soon took it, with the result that she opened his letters and followed him from town to town, not in his company, but dogging his footsteps. She plagued him at his meetings and tried to injure him in every possible way.

Of her Southey remarks :

> By her outrageous jealousy and abominable temper, she deserves to be classed in a triad with Xantippe and the wife of Job, as one of the three bad wives.

185

Though Wesley was not a man to allow bitter feelings to overcome him, he at last wrote her a letter in which he told her exactly what he thought of her.   He said :

> Know me, and know yourself. Suspect me no more, asperse me no more, provoke me no more : do not any longer contend for mastery, for power, money, or praise : be content to be a private, insignificant person, known and loved by God and me.
>
> Of what importance is your character to mankind ?   If you were buried just now, or if you had never lived, what loss would it be to the cause of God ?

For twenty years Wesley was pestered by his wife. At last she left his house, taking away all his papers, which he never saw again.

Whereupon he wrote in his diary, as if it were merely a passing comment, recording the fact that she had gone, declaring that he did not know the reason for her desertion, and adding :

> I did not forsake her, I did not dismiss her, I will not recall her.

She lived ten years after she had left him and died in 1781 in Camberwell, where a stone records that " she was a woman of exemplary virtue, a tender parent, and a sincere friend."

Another of Wesley's failures in life—and there were few—was his boarding-school for boys at Kingswood, near Bristol.

Wesley could not see the need for recreation, and imposed upon the boys eight hours for sleep, eight hours for study, and eight hours for meals.

Of course, the meals did not take the full eight hours, but the surplus above the actual eating time was set apart for prayer, meditation, singing, and working.

A master would always keep a wary eye on the boys and prevent idle talk and laziness.

JOHN WESLEY PREACHING AT A MARKET-CROSS

W. Hatherell

186

No holidays were allowed, because Wesley believed that the good work that had been done at the school would have been in vain if the boys were to be away for any lengthy period.

His refusal to understand the reason for the school's failure is inexplicable in a man of Wesley's type.

Masters were changed, and scholars were expelled, but still the rules were broken, and he had to confess that this method of turning out young recruits for the ministry did not work.

As a leader Wesley had remarkable powers. It was his own example which his followers obeyed, and they did not spare themselves. Wesley himself was content to submit to any self-abnegation.

For fifty years he rose at four in the morning, summer and winter, and preached a sermon at five. Start early and they would keep the flock together, he always maintained, and not an hour of the day was wasted. Whenever they dropped this rigorous routine it would be the death of Methodism.

" Though I am always in haste," he said, " I am never in a hurry, because I never undertake any more work than I can go through with perfect calmness of spirit." He continued :

> It is true I travel 4000 or 5000 miles in a year, but I generally travel alone in my carriage, and am as retired ten hours a day as if I were in a wilderness. On other days I never spend less than three hours, and frequently ten or twelve, alone.

For many years he never tasted animal food, and for one period of three or four years lived solely on potatoes. He was always in good health, and never lost a night's sleep. Almost to the day of his death he had a clear complexion and an agile walk.

In his old age he was a picturesque figure with his long white hair and smiling countenance, and when he died he had no disease. He lay down his head and died—worn out.

Wesley was a voluminous writer, and the money he obtained in this way through his own printing-press he gave away—about £30,000.

He always lived within his means whatever his income. At Oxford he received £30 a year, spent £28, and gave £2 away. Another year his income being £60, he was able to give away £32. Always limiting himself to £28, he was able year by year to allocate more and more to charity.

John Wesley, born on June 17, 1703, was a son of a clergyman of the Established Church, and was the brother of Charles and Samuel Wesley.

At an early age he was sent to Charterhouse School, and in his seventeenth year entered Christ Church, Oxford. He obtained a fellowship in Lincoln College in 1726, and soon afterwards was appointed Greek lecturer.

He became a deacon in 1725, and then officiated as curate to his father at Wroote, remaining two years and being ordained priest.

He was thirty-five before he began to do anything more than an ordinary parson. On May 14, 1738, after he had been to America on a missionary excursion to the Indians, he went, as he describes, " very unwillingly " to a meeting in Aldersgate Street, where he heard some one reading Luther's preface to the Epistle to the Romans.

" At about a quarter before nine o'clock light flashed upon my mind, and I was converted." Until that time he admitted he had never known what Christianity meant.

Following the procedure of Whitefield, he began to preach in the open air. The two worked well in conjunction, until they became divided on points of doctrine.

They both met at a meeting-place in Fetter Lane, which was eventually the cradle of Methodism, but there was a strange difference between the two styles of preaching.

Whitefield, it is said, touched the hearts, while Wesley " gave rise to those bodily excitements which so long continued to throw perplexity and discredit upon Methodism, such as it was under his guidance."

The most depraved of men wept as they listened to Whitefield ; in Wesley's early years he was interrupted by convulsions and epileptic seizures. Excesses gradually ceased, however, and Wesleyan Methodism became a great and powerful institution.

Wesley and Whitefield parted company in 1741. By this time there were chapels in many of the large towns of England, in which services were held either by ordained or non-ordained preachers.

Often the lay preachers were subjected to persecution by mobs egged on by magistrates or even clergymen of the Church of England. At times Wesley barely escaped with his life.

In 1744 John and Charles Wesley met four clergymen and four lay preachers to hold " a conference." Thus was the Methodist Conference instituted.

Wesley died on March 2, 1791, in the eighty-eighth year of his life and the sixty-fifth year of his ministry.

In the early part of his campaign Wesley stood zealously by the tenets of the Established Church. Later, on the persuasion of Dr Thomas Coke, an Oxford man and an ordained clergyman, who devoted his private fortune to the cause, Wesley reluctantly took the only course which would result in the consolidation of his society. He conferred ordination upon some of the preachers.

At length, also, he sanctioned the administration of

the sacraments in his chapels, and made his preachers clergymen, thus turning his society into a Church.

It was a blow to him when his followers decided upon separation from the Established Church, and it was a long time before he would give way to the clamour of ministers and people for liberty to preach, to worship, and to act without the authority of the Established Church.

Not until 1784 did Wesleyan Methodism reach a status as a religious community, with a proper organization, by the legal constitution of the Conference as a responsible body and the legal proprietor of the chapels and other chattels of the society.

In 1790 the community numbered 76,000 in Great Britain and 57,000 in America.

XXXIII

The Delusions of Jean-Jacques Rousseau

THOUGH Jean-Jacques Rousseau posed as an authority on domestic affairs, he was never able to steer clear of entanglements himself.

One of his problems was Thérèse le Vasseur, whom he met at an inn at which he was staying in Paris. Thérèse was a servant at the inn, and when he first met her in 1743 she had no education, understanding, or beauty.

She had a mother who was the bane of Rousseau's life.

In the course of a few years Thérèse is supposed to have given birth to five children, of whom Rousseau was the father.

But there is a doubt whether she had any children. Rousseau never saw them.

According to Thérèse, they were deposited at the foundling hospital. Certainly Rousseau was very little concerned about them, and disregarded all responsibility.

Some of Rousseau's contemporaries declared that the five babies were fictions, invented by Thérèse and her mother to make the tie between Thérèse and Rousseau more binding.

Before this affair there were others which began when he was only sixteen.

Rousseau was born at Geneva in June, 1712. His father was a watchmaker, his mother the daughter of a minister. When he was ten his father had to skip away from Geneva owing to a dispute with a fellow-citizen which caused a short term of imprisonment.

The boy was taken over by relatives, and at the age of twelve was apprenticed to a notary. His master thought him incapable, and he was apprenticed afresh to an engraver.

In 1728 he ran away from his home at Lyons. He had returned to the city after the gates were shut. Being unable to get in, he decided to stay out altogether.

According to his *Confessions*, he wandered about until he found a protector at Annecy in Mme de Warens, a young and pretty widow. This arrangement, however, was temporary, and he roamed about in Turin, at last obtaining a post as a footman to a Mme de Vercellis.

There, it is said, he stole a piece of ribbon, and, when inquiries were made, blamed a girl fellow-servant.

Soon afterwards his mistress died. He obtained another situation with the Comte de Gouvon, but was soon dismissed.

He returned to Mme de Warens, and became ostensibly a servant but really a lover. She arranged for his education to be completed, but his roving disposition again asserted itself, and he disappeared. When he returned to Annecy again he found that Mme de Warens had gone.

For some months, according to his *Confessions*, he wandered about trying to earn a living by giving lessons in music, a subject of which he knew little. He then became secretary to a Greek travelling in Switzerland, and later got to Paris through the introduction of the French Ambassador at Soleure.

While there he heard that Mme Warens was at Chambéry. He sought her out and was installed again in her household. On his account she took a country-house, where they lived in the summer, spending the winter in Paris.

In 1738 his health broke down, and he went to Montpelier.   He appears to have picked up on the way a Mme de Larnage, with whom he lived while recuperating.

When he returned to Mme de Warens he found that she had another man in her house.   Rousseau had to play second fiddle.   He very soon left to become tutor to some children at Lyons, but quickly lost this position.

In 1740 he went back to Mme de Warens' country-house, to find that the situation there had not changed. He then gave up trying to regain the lady's favour.

After holding various other posts, he went to Paris, and began to earn a living copying music.   Staying at the Hotel St Quentin, he arranged for himself a domestic establishment with Thérèse le Vasseur.

He was happy with her, except for the interference by her mother.

He began to contribute to various periodicals, and in a few years made his mark as a writer.

The Academy of Dijon offered a prize for an essay on the effect of the progress of civilization on morals.

Rousseau won the prize and became famous.

Society began to demand his company, and with this backing he brought out in 1752 an operetta which was successful.   He received a hundred louis for it and was requested to appear at Court, but he was too shy to do so.

During a visit to Geneva in 1754 he met his old love, Mme de Warens.   She was reduced in circumstances and attractions, and Rousseau did not linger in her company.

Returning to Paris, he became friendly with Mme d'Epinay, who fitted up a cottage for him.   He stayed there a year and wrote *La Nouvelle Héloïse*, becoming devoted to the sister of his patroness.   The young lady

13

had a husband and a lover, but Rousseau appears to have gained her favour.

It was at the cottage that his petulance caused a quarrel between Diderot, Frederick Melchior Grimm, and himself. It is said that the dispute was really due to Rousseau's refusal to cover up Mme d'Epinay's affair with Grimm. He left the cottage and went to live in the neighbourhood.

Although his personal behaviour was bringing him many enemies, his writings brought him friends.

His work *Emile* caused Parliament to threaten him with imprisonment. In 1762 he escaped to Switzerland, where he remained some years. At last the clergy caused the peasantry to rise against him, and he returned to Paris.

David Hume, the historian, then in Paris, pitied Rousseau and invited him to come to London. He landed in England in January, 1766. Thérèse followed him, and she was entrusted to the charge of James Boswell.

Rousseau was lionized in London, but he could not make up his mind whether he was pleased with his reception or not.

In the summer of 1770 he returned to Paris and resumed music-copying. He had by this time gone through a form of marriage with Thérèse.

There is no doubt that Rousseau was mostly insane. Throughout his life he had believed that he had secret enemies, and this feeling became intensified in later life.

He died on July 2, 1778, but the circumstances of his death are not known. There are stories that he shot himself, poisoned himself, and that he died of apoplexy.

XXXIV

FREDERICK "THE BRAINLESS"—AFTERWARDS "THE GREAT"

FREDERICK THE GREAT, King of Prussia, had no brains as a youth. At least, that was the opinion of his father, the elder Frederick, who declared : "My eldest son is a coxcomb, proud, and has a fine French spirit that spoils all my plans."

Frederick William I brought up his son with extreme severity so that he might become a great soldier and " acquire thrift and frugality."

This procedure was not at all to the liking of young Frederick. He detested the military exercises which he was compelled to undergo, and preferred the tuition which he received from a Frenchwoman, Mme de Roucoulle, which mainly concerned literature, a subject for which the coarse King had little use.

In addition, Frederick acquired a taste for music, learned Latin secretly, against the wishes of his father, derided religion, and refused to learn to ride and shoot.

He despised German habits, and his feelings were shared by his sister, Wilhelmina.

The life of young Frederick was one of continuous antagonism to his father, who introduced a regimen for the boy with the object of breaking his spirit.

One day the boy was seen playing the flute accompanied on the piano by a young girl. The girl was publicly flogged through the streets of Potsdam by the executioner.

At last the Queen decided that the time had come to take action, and made arrangements for him to seek refuge in England with George II. Only the boy's sister and two lieutenants were in the plot for smuggling him to England.

The King heard of it, and finding that the boy had already left the palace, sent soldiers after him, and he was caught just as he was entering his carriage to take him to Saxony.

One of the lieutenants escaped, but the other was brought back to Potsdam, handcuffed to the Prince. Each was thrown in a separate dungeon, and when Wilhelmina implored her father to release her brother, she was thrown from one of the palace windows.

The King had now firmly made up his mind that his son would die on the scaffold, and believed that such a fate for his offspring would be an intervention of Providence for the security of the country.

He was certain that his son would be no good. " He will always be a disobedient subject," he said, " and I have three other boys who are more than his equals."

So the father prepared to execute his son.

The captured lieutenant was sentenced by court-martial to imprisonment for life. The King, however, changed the sentence to one of death, and the lieutenant was executed in Frederick's presence.

At last the Prince was saved by the intercession of the Emperor of Austria, Charles VI.

It was then reported by the prison chaplain that the Prince had now had a change of heart. He was released from solitary confinement and sent to work in the auditing office of the Departments of War and Agriculture at Cüstrin while the pardon was being granted.

" The whole town shall be his prison," the King

wrote, " and I will give him employment from morning to night in the Departments of War and Agriculture and of the Government." He added :

> He shall work at financial matters, receive accounts, read minutes, and make extracts. . . . But if he kicks or rears again, he shall forfeit the succession to the Crown, and even, according to circumstances, life itself.

Frederick, unknown to his father, fell in love with Amelia, the daughter of George II. His father, who had actually arranged for him to marry her, then cancelled the marriage because the Prince had been in correspondence with the English court.

In addition he cancelled the marriage that had been arranged between his daughter, Wilhelmina, and the Prince of Wales.

Young Frederick gradually fell in with his father's wishes. He began to see there was no option, his father being determined to have his own way. On November 30, 1731, he was allowed to appear in uniform, and in the following year he became a colonel of the regiment at Neuruppin.

In 1733 he married the Princess Elizabeth Christina, daughter of the Duke of Brunswick-Bevern.

He was granted the estate of Rheinsberg, near Neuruppin, and although the marriage which had been arranged for him by his father was an unhappy one, he was more content than he had been at any period of his life.

He and his wife lived apart, and it is said he treated her very harshly and brutally.

He became King on May 31, 1740, and began to rule with much more feeling than his father. All religious opinions were allowed, torture was abolished, treason cases were conducted with strict justice. While he ruled himself, he would always allow people to state their wrong personally to him.

When the Emperor Charles VI died in 1740, he immediately made military preparations for the conquest of the three Silesian duchies which Prussia had always asserted were hers by right.

He invaded Silesia with an army of 30,000 and gained a victory against the Austrians at Mollwitz. Being under the impression the battle was lost, he left the field early, which gave rise to the belief that he lacked courage.

A second victory was gained at Chotusitz in May, 1742, and Maria Theresa agreed to the Peace of Breslau which put Frederick in possession of Silesia. When the Prince of Friesland died without heirs he also took over that country.

At the age of thirty-three Frederick was the most important sovereign of his time. He administered the country himself, his ministers being puppets.

The economic development of Prussia continued apace. Agriculture improved, the burden of the peasants was lightened, and the army was increased to 160,000 men.

He lived alone in a mansion which he gave the name of *Sans Souci*, and rose regularly in the summer at five, and in the winter at six, devoting himself to public business until eleven.

From 1756 to 1763 his energies were directed to the conduct of the Seven Years' War, in which he pitted his strength against almost the whole of Europe.

Though the resources of the country were sadly depleted by this war, he was able, through the peace of Hubertushof, to maintain the status of Prussia, and to obtain recognition for Prussia as one of the great powers of the Continent.

From this time it was inevitable that there would

be a final struggle between Prussia and Austria for the supremacy.

Immediately after the conclusion of peace, Frederick set about putting the country in order to enable it to recover from the terrible loss it had sustained.

Some States were relieved of taxation for a period, big landowners were given free issues of corn to replace that which had been destroyed, and a great deal of money was spent in the erection of new houses to replace those razed to the ground.

The coinage was restored to its proper value, and the Bank of Berlin was founded.

His excise was on French lines, and while the system resulted in a big revenue, there was much corruption by the French officials. This resulted in criticism of the King, which he took in good part.

One day, while riding along the Jäger Strasse, he came upon a crowd of people.

Turning to the groom, he said : " See what it is."

" They have something posted up about your Majesty," reported the groom.

Riding up to the poster, the King found a caricature of himself in " melancholy guise, seated on a stool, a coffee-mill between his knees, diligently grinding with the one hand, and with the other picking up any bean that might have fallen."

" Hang it lower," said the King. He beckoned his groom and ordered him to lower the poster, " so that they may not have to hurt their necks about it."

The result was exactly as the King had anticipated. The crowd gave him a hearty cheer, tore the caricature into pieces, and as the King rode away cried out, " Frederick for ever ! "

The King was scrupulous in the administration of justice, although he disliked formality.

In one case, described as " the miller Arnold case," he dismissed the judges and condemned them to a year's imprisonment in a fortress, because he considered that they had not done justice to a poor man.

He liked to be described as the advocate of the poor, and was greatly pleased at the answer given to him by a miller whose windmill stood on ground which was required for the King's garden.

The miller refused to sell it. " Not at any price ? " suggested the King's agent. " Could not the King take it from you for nothing if he chose ? "

" Have we not the Kammergericht (Court of Appeal) at Berlin ? " was the retort, and this became a popular saying.

Frederick died at *Sans Souci* on August 17, 1786, through exposure to rain during a military review. He left Prussia in a much stronger position than when he began to reign.

The treasury was full and the army considerably increased in strength.

He was careless of his personal appearance, was somewhat stout and below medium height. During his later years he was content with an old blue military uniform, the breast of which was usually browned with snuff.

XXXV

GENERAL JAMES WOLFE, " MAD " HERO OF QUEBEC

THE storming of the Heights of Abraham was one of the most hare-brained exploits in the history of Britain.

When George II was told that it was the act of a madman, he retorted, " Mad, was he ? Then I wish he were alive to bite some of my generals."

If Wolfe was not mad, he was certainly eccentric.

A striking example of his mentality was his reaction to the decision of Pitt to entrust him with the Canadian expedition.

It was the evening before the General's embarkation, and he, together with William Pitt and Lord Temple, sat dining at Pitt's house at Hayes. Wolfe had received final instructions on the campaign from Pitt, when suddenly he jumped up from the table, drew his sword, and began to flourish it to the great consternation of the two Ministers.

But that was not all. Wolfe, in a loud voice, declared that his sword would carve a way through the enemy. This exhibition from a hitherto apparently mild-mannered young man so astounded the two Ministers that, for a time, they were struck speechless.

When Wolfe had gone from the house, and the noise of his carriage wheels had faded into the distance, Pitt, fearing that he had made a fatal error of judgment in entrusting Wolfe with the expedition, exclaimed to Lord

Temple : " Good God ! that I should have entrusted the fate of the country and of the administration to such hands ! "

Lord Temple afterwards declared that Wolfe had taken practically no wine that evening, so that his ebullition was not due to alcohol.

The incident illustrates how a shy man may, under the influence of emotion, become bombastic, and confirms Wolfe's own statement that there were times when he lapsed from his usual attitude of reserve.

Some biographers of Wolfe attempt to link him up with the scandalous atrocities of the Duke of Cumberland following the battle of Culloden Moor in 1746. In his misapplied zeal in stamping out the Jacobite rising the commander of the English forces placed Jacobite prisoners, whether wounded or not, against a wall and had them shot. Houses and villages were burned, crops and stock destroyed.

There was a Wolfe who was either a major or a captain in Cumberland's army, and there is good reason to believe he was the person who afterwards became the general. It is known that he received a captain's commission in June, 1744, in Barrell's regiment, which stood at the left of the front line of the Hanoverians at Culloden.

Efforts have been made either to associate or dissociate Wolfe with these atrocities, without any definite result, although it is known that his earliest letter home from Scotland is dated January, 1749, three years after the failure of the Jacobite Rising.

Wolfe was born in 1727 at Westerham, Kent, and was the elder son of Lieut.-colonel Edward Wolfe. He was educated at private schools, first at Westerham and then at Greenwich. As a child he was not strong, but a determination to become a soldier eventually led to a commission in the Royal Marines in 1741. Then, being transferred to a line regiment, he was sent to Flanders in the spring of 1742 as an ensign in the 12th Foot. He served in the battles of Dettingen, Falkirk, presumably Culloden, and Laffeldt, where he was wounded.

In 1749 he was appointed Acting-Commander of the 20th Foot, rose to Lieutenant-colonel the following year, remaining with this regiment for eight years while it was stationed at several towns in Scotland, and from 1753 at various places in the south of England.

In 1757 he was appointed Quartermaster-general in Ireland, and in 1758 served as brigadier under Amherst in the force entrusted with the expedition against Cape Breton and Quebec. He was particularly noted for his service at the siege of Louisbourg.

When he was given command of the new expedition to renew the attack on Quebec, and although technically under Amherst, he was to use his own discretion as to the conduct of the operations.

Leaving England in 1759, the expedition sailed 300 miles up the St Lawrence and disembarked on the Isle of Orleans, and encamped facing the city.

The French were in command of Montcalm, as intrepid a soldier as Wolfe, and were superior in numbers, although a part of their force consisted of irregulars. Their defences were exceedingly strong.

Wolfe began the attack by seizing Point Lévis, a position from which the city was bombarded, but the artillery fire did little damage to the main defences of Quebec, which was protected on one side by the St Lawrence, on another by the St Charles, and on the third side of the triangle by the Plains of Abraham, an impregnable position with, it was thought, no approach from the sea.

After some weeks of waiting Wolfe was foiled in his attempt to cross the St Lawrence seven miles below

Quebec, and while the defenders could not be lured from their positions the situation remained very much the same.

On July 31 Wolfe attacked from the Montmorency River, which runs into the St Lawrence four miles below Quebec, but was repulsed with heavy loss, and it was evident that this position was too strongly defended to leave any hope of success.

Above the city the northern shores of the river were steep, and it was also impossible to reduce Quebec by gunfire. Wolfe despaired of success, and in his messages to England he emphasized the possibility of failure, particularly as unfavourable weather would soon be encountered. When Wolfe fell ill, hopes of a successful expedition dropped to zero.

All these reports created an unfavourable impression in England. Then suddenly, when every one was preparing to hear news of the return of the expedition, the tidings were received that Quebec had fallen and Wolfe had been killed.

It is believed that Wolfe's brigadiers suggested the possibility of climbing the heights on the left bank of the river above Quebec. It was thought that it would be just possible to cut off the French supplies, which had to be brought from the interior over the high land or during the night along the river in boats.

As darkness fell on the night of September 12, when it was expected that the convoys with the enemy's supplies would be brought down the river, several boats left the British ships filled with troops, and they gradually drifted down with the tide.

Wolfe could spare only 3600 men for the attack, because of the loss of so many effectives through illness. Challenged by the sentinels, the English answered in French, and they were allowed to pass unmolested. They disembarked at what is now known as Wolfe's Cove, whence a path ran up the hill to the heights.

The path was guarded by a redoubt, but the light infantry used for scaling the hill scrambled up wherever they could find a foothold. In support of this sally the English fleet kept up a bombardment of Montcalm's main position, and thus distracted the Frenchmen's attention.

Hands as well as feet were required to negotiate the slopes. The garrison of the redoubt, startled by the attack, gave up their work. Up went Wolfe and his men, and by daybreak they were lined up on the heights, level with the upper works of Quebec.

Montcalm had been detained by the demonstration by the fleet, but he now realized that the real attack was coming on his other flank, and so he hurried all the troops he could over the St Charles, drawing them up on the plain with their backs to the wall of the upper town.

Montcalm had plenty of militiamen and irregulars, and he decided to attack at once. It was fortunate for Wolfe that he decided to fight rather than withstand a siege. No doubt the Frenchman was anxious about the arrival of English reinforcements, and the possibility of artillery being dragged by bluejackets up the cliff.

Whatever may have been Montcalm's reason there was no doubt that it proved the reason of his defeat.

Wolfe's men were not long in realizing that the enemy were in much superior force, but with his personal example he steadied them, and, waiting until the French came within range, they fired a volley with deadly effect.

The French stopped with big gaps in their ranks, and Wolfe led his men on to victory. While advancing, Wolfe was killed, and Montcalm received a wound which caused him to ride into Quebec at an early stage of the battle. He died on September 18, before the British troops entered the city.

The battle decided the supremacy of the English in Canada. Wolfe had been wounded twice earlier in the battle, but had refused to leave the field. His death-wound was caused by a bullet which passed through his lungs.

While he was lying, apparently unconscious, some one near him cried out : " They run : see how they run ! "

" Who run ? " demanded Wolfe, rousing himself.

" The enemy," was the reply. " They give way everywhere."

Lifting himself upon his hands, he gave his final order for cutting off the French retreat, and fell back mur-muring : " Now, God be praised, I will die in peace."

On the spot where the battle was fought there stands a tall column bearing the words : " Here died Wolfe victorious on the 13th September, 1759."

In the garden of the Governor at Quebec there is a monument to the memory of Wolfe and his gallant foe, Montcalm.

A public memorial was unveiled to Wolfe in West-minster Abbey on October 4, 1773, and his body was brought to England and buried at Greenwich.

XXXVI

EDMUND BURKE'S OBSESSIONS

EDMUND BURKE, the great parliamentarian of the eighteenth century, had an obsession which not only prejudiced his political career but lost him a friend of many years' standing.

The fear of Napoleon would intrude itself upon Burke's mind to such an extent that in parliamentary debates upon entirely different subjects his speech would veer round and become a diatribe against the French revolutionists.

It was a memorable scene in the House of Commons when Burke and Charles James Fox, who might have been described as the Whig twins, had a verbal duel which ended in Burke's declaring that their friendship was ended.

Burke was never really popular in the House of Commons, for his speeches were often delivered with a ferocity that disturbed the equanimity of the assembly.

The Revolution in France was generally welcomed by the Whig leaders, such as Fox and Sheridan, but Burke was its most bitter antagonist. He and Sheridan fell out soon after the outbreak of the Revolution in 1789.

His friendly relations with Fox, which had extended over a period of twenty years, had already been prejudiced on the same grounds months before the tornado burst upon the House of Commons.

During a debate on the Quebec Bill, Fox thought it

necessary to sneer at the Revolution. Burke was not in the House, but heard of it and determined to reply.

Next day the " twins," who, in private life, were still good friends, walked together arm in arm from Burke's house in Duke Street down to Westminster. Outwardly there was nothing to show that Burke was furious.

The debate on the Quebec Bill was resumed, and at once Burke got on to his feet and began to express his usual condemnation of the Jacobins. There followed an angry debate between Pitt, Grey, Lord Sheffield, and others concerning the merits of the Revolution.

At last a resolution was proposed confining the debate to the proper subject, and this was seconded by Fox. He taxed Burke with inconsistency, and threw in his face words which Burke had previously used about the insurgent American colonists.

Burke in reply declared that this was a deliberate attack on him, detailed Fox's inconsistencies, and pointed out the many disagreements between them in the House of Commons, adding that such disagreements had not broken their friendship.

Whatever it might entail, however it might prejudice friendship, Burke declared, he would go on and on warning the country against the French Revolution.

" But there is no loss of friends, I hope," said Fox eagerly, in a voice that was meant for Burke only.

" Yes," replied Burke, " there *is* a loss of friends. I know the penalty of my conduct. I have done my duty at the price of my friend—our friendship is at an end."

Fox staggered to his feet, but for some minutes he was so overcome he could not speak. Then, with his eyes streaming with tears, he implored Burke to reconsider. A twenty years' friendship should not be sacrificed for political reasons.

But Burke could not be shaken ; to him the danger of the French Revolution was such that every other consideration should be thrust aside.

This rift between the two friends was never bridged, and when Burke and Fox were called upon to meet upon other matters their attitude was one of strict formality.

If Burke took a more serious view of the Revolution than any other parliamentarian, the prophecies which he had uttered from time to time in the House of Commons were fulfilled.

The violence of the Paris mob increased, the Jacobins took the place of the more moderate revolutionaries. They flooded the Tuileries, the Swiss Guard was massacred, the Royal Family put under restraint, and the King and Queen were executed.

These horrors stirred the imagination of the English people, and efforts were made to get the Government to intervene.

England declared war against the French Republic, with Fox stoutly opposing it, and Burke hoping that some new excess across the Channel would at length cause the Whig leader to change his opinions.

War to the death with the leaders of the Revolution was the policy of Burke.

If Burke set his hand to the plough he never drew back. That characteristic was seen in his impeachment of Warren Hastings for alleged crimes and misdemeanours in his government of India.

Other members, notably Sheridan, said enough against Hastings to paint him a villain of the deepest dye, but when Burke got on to his feet and let out a flood of verbal vindictiveness, the usual cool and intrepid Hastings squirmed and cried out in protest like a criminal in the rack.

Burke's somewhat exaggerated sense of justice did

14

more than anything else to sweep away corruption in the administration of India.

Although Hastings was acquitted in 1795, after the matter had been a first-class political sensation for nine years, the assiduity with which Burke pursued it to the end did lasting good to Indian affairs.

Not a great deal is known of the early life of Burke, but he is believed to have been born on January 12, 1729, some say in Dublin and others in London. His father was a Protestant and his mother a Catholic. His earliest schoolmaster was a member of the Society of Friends.

In 1743 he entered Trinity College, Dublin, took his degree in 1748, and then came to London to study law. In 1756 he is believed to have lived in the Temple, and became friendly with many of the notabilities of the day, including Garrick, Reynolds, and Johnson.

For the next few years he earned his living by writing, and soon became well known in society.

In 1765 he was appointed private secretary to the Marquess of Rockingham, who had just been made Prime Minister. At this time Burke appears to have made enemies who tried to secure his dismissal by Rockingham, but his employer, noting Burke's attitude under the accusations, refused to believe them.

In 1765 he was returned for the pocket borough of Wendover, and soon became active in the House, speaking on the American question and actually against his party.

His voice was harsh, he had awkward actions, but he was regarded as one of the most powerful advocates of the day. Gradually he became indispensable to his party, and in 1774 began his famous alliance with Charles James Fox, who was then a youth of twenty-five.

He was ardent in his attempts at conciliation in connexion with the American trouble.

All the time he received the friendship of Rockingham and was placed in various posts. While he was Paymaster of the Forces in the Portland Ministry he first took an interest in Indian affairs.

At that time he was treated with marked contempt by the House, and was often jeered at and received with interruptions. His first attack on Hastings was not received with approval by the members.

When the impeachment of Hastings ended in 1795, Burke retired from Parliament. He was granted a pension, and the King was desirous of making him a peer. His title was to be Lord Beaconsfield.

The patent was being got ready when suddenly Burke's son died, and this so broke the old man that he refused the title in a most pathetic speech :

> The storm has gone over me, and I lie like one of those old oaks which the late hurricane has scattered about me. I am stripped of all my honours ; I am torn up by the roots and lie prostrate on the earth. . . . I am alone.
>
> I have none to meet my enemies in the gate. . . . I live in an inverted order. They who ought to have succeeded me have gone before me. They who should have been to me as posterity are in the place of ancestors.

All he would accept was a pension of £2500. Remarks were made in Parliament regarding the paltry reward to a man who, in conducting a great trial on the public behalf, had worked harder for nearly ten years than any minister in any cabinet of the reign.

But Burke was not finished. In 1796 he published his *Letters on a Regicide Peace*, probably the greatest of his compositions. Pitt was anxious for peace with France to stop the waste of public money. The public debt had swollen to 400 millions.

Burke opposed negotiation, and his letters stirred the country as never before. When the third of these publications came into the hands of the people Burke had died, on July 9, 1797.

Fox proposed a public funeral, and that he should be buried in Westminster Abbey, but Burke had left strict injunctions that he should be buried at Beaconsfield, and here he was laid to rest, some of his old Whig friends— and enemies—following behind his coffin.

Though the Western world was rent with war and rapine, the death of Burke was summed up in the following words : " There is but one event, but that is an event for the world—Burke is dead."

XXXVII

George Washington, First American President

THE story of George Washington, the cherry tree, and the hatchet has probably little truth in it.

No doubt George could tell a " fib " as readily as any other American boy.

Weems, the biographer of Washington, has no moral anecdotes of the great George in his 1800 biography. Six years later, in his more comprehensive work, there were many.

Thus it seems likely that Weems introduced the stories for embellishment.

As a boy, Washington was backward in his studies. Mathematics was his chief subject, and although he was continually in contact with the French element in his district, he failed to acquire the language.

The future first President of the United States was born at Bridges Creek, Westmorland County, Virginia, on February 22, 1732. The family is believed to have been connected with the Washingtons of Sulgrave, Northamptonshire, England, for a John and Lawrence Washington appeared in Virginia in 1658, John taking up property at Bridges Creek. He became a member of the House of Burgesses in 1666, and died in 1676. Later the family changed their residence to Virginia.

It is possible to follow George's career from the time he left school in the autumn of 1747. The story is told that a commission as midshipman in the English Navy was offered to George by Admiral Edward Vernon, and that his mother opposed the idea ; but there is no substantiation of it.

Certain it is, however, that at sixteen he became a surveyor of the plantation property of William Fairfax, a kinsman of the family. Later he held a post as public surveyor for three years, and acquired a disposition to speculate in real estate.

Not long after this he inherited the extensive Mount Vernon property following the death of his half-brother, Lawrence.

It was in 1753 that he had his first official task. He was chosen by Governor Robert Dinwiddie to warn the French away from their new posts on the Ohio. Next year, as Lieutenant-colonel of a Virginia regiment, under Colonel Joshua Fry, he defeated a force of French and Indians at Great Meadows, Pennsylvania.

Two months later, however, he was forced to capitulate after a stubborn defence, but received the thanks of the House of Burgesses.

In February, 1755, Washington wrote to General Edward Braddock, who had just arrived in Virginia, offering his services, and was made a member of his staff with the rank of colonel. There followed the great defeat of Braddock by the Indians.

During the whole of the battle, Washington, unruffled, rode along the lines on horseback rallying the troops, a conspicuous target for the Indian bullets. He actually saved the expedition from complete annihiliation.

After his return in August he became Commander of the Virginian forces at the age of twenty-three, and for two years was defending a frontier 350 miles long with only 700 men. This task was rendered more difficult by insubordination and official restrictions and inter- ference. In 1757 his health broke down, but the follow- ing year he was in command of the advance guard of the

GEORGE WASHINGTON
Adolf Ulrik Wertmüller

214

expedition under General John Forbes, which occupied Fort Duquesne and renamed it Fort Pitt.

Towards the end of the year the war ended, and he resigned his commission and married Martha Dandridge, widow of Daniel Park Custis.

The next fifteen years of Washington's life were spent as a planter in Virginia. He was prosperous, a member of the Established Church, employed many slaves, although he was always a considerate master, and he was prominent in the affairs of the State.

As time went on, Washington lost the reputation he had gained at the battle in which Braddock was defeated. In his quiet life in Virginia the glamour evaporated.

He was one of the richest men in the colonies ; and with the 100,000 dollars which his wife had brought him as her dowry he continued developing his already vast estates. He was always a member of the House of Burgesses, but he never appears to have made any important speeches, contenting himself with a mere expression of opinion. Neither does he appear to have had any advanced views concerning the slave problem. He employed them himself, and no doubt considered that it was quite the right thing to do.

He first showed some real interest in affairs on the famous occasion when Patrick Henry introduced his resolutions against the Stamp Act, and four years later is found taking a definite line on the Philadelphia non-importation resolutions, and hinting that force might finally be necessary against the ministry.

In the following May the House of Burgesses was dissolved, and he was one of the members who met at the Raleigh tavern and adopted a non-importation agreement, he himself keeping the agreement when the others failed. As matters between England and the colony became worse, Washington even opposed petitions to the

King and Parliament on the ground that the colonists should not whine for relief.

Washington's career as a nationalist began in August, 1774, when he was appointed by the Virginia convention as one of the seven delegates to the first Continental Congress. By this time he had no doubt in his own mind that the struggle against taxation would lead to open war.

" More blood will be spilled on this occasion," he said, " if the ministry are determined to push matters to extremity, than history has e~er yet furnished instances of in the annals of North America."

His military ability was recognized, and there is no doubt that Congress had him in view in the event of hostilities breaking out. Nevertheless, he hesitated before declaring himself on the side of the revolutionaries.

The war began in Massachusetts, and Washington was chosen by Virginia. Congress then decided that the armed forces of the colonies should be put in a position of defence, and Washington became the Commander-in-chief of the United States.

He refused a salary, asking only for expenses, declaring at the same time that he did not believe himself to be equal to the command, and that he accepted it only because of the unanimity of Congress.

On June 17, 1775, he set out for Cambridge (Mass.) and took command of the troops assembled for action against the British garrison in Boston. He planned expeditions against Canada and sent out privateers to harass British shipping. On the conclusion of peace in 1783, with America independent, Washington urged " an indissoluble union of the States under one Federal head," the adoption of a suitable military establishment during peace.

The army was discontented ; the soldiers had not

received their pay, and it was with some difficulty that Washington settled the dispute.

The Society of the Cincinnati, an organization composed of officers of the late war, chose him as President, and when the Federal Convention met at Philadelphia in May, 1787, to frame a constitution, he was present as delegate for Virginia. A unanimous vote made him president officer much against his will, and although he was unable to take part in the debate he approved the constitution as drawn up and signed it, keeping the papers of the Convention until the adoption of the new Government.

His influence was decisive in getting ratification of the constitution, and when the time came to elect a president there was no quibbling. As one delegate said, the office had been " cut to fit the measure of George Washington," and no one opposed his election, which was effected by the unanimous vote of the electors.

He was returned in 1792–3, and even after he had definitely refused to stand for a third term, two electors voted for him in 1796–7.

Washington's chief fault was his failure to appreciate the necessity for party government, and in selecting persons of different views to form his first Cabinet he was unwittingly sowing the seeds of trouble, for Alexander Hamilton and Thomas Jefferson, of opposite political doctrines, were like " two gamecocks in a pit."

Washington's proclamation of neutrality in the war between England and France caused much anger among his political opponents, and alienated the partisans of France. Like many other public men in the eighteenth century, he was the object of much scandal and slander.

Letters were forged and published purporting to show that he had held a desire to abandon the revolutionary struggle. He was accused of drawing more than his salary. It was said that his manners were conceited in that he had aped monarchy, and the suggestion was actually made that he should be guillotined.

These attacks induced him to remark, even during his first Presidency : " I would rather be in my grave than in my present position," and further that " he had never repented but once the having slipped the moment of resigning his office, and that was every moment since."

He retired from the Presidency in 1797 and returned to Mount Vernon, being met everywhere on the way with demonstrations of affection. It was about this time that he resolved never to employ another slave, and wished that he could persuade Virginia to abolish slavery.

Washington died quietly. Just before his end, he felt his own pulse, and his countenance changed. The physician placed his hand over the eyes of the dying man, and he died " without a struggle or a sigh."

XXXVIII

James Watt and the Kettle

"I NEVER saw such an idle boy," said Mrs Muirhead, the aunt of James Watt.

"Take a book, or employ yourself usefully. For the last hour you have not spoken one word, but taken off the lid of that kettle and put it on again."

Mrs Muirhead did not live to see what effect this trifling with the kettle would produce in the inventive mind of young Watt.

A practical woman, she was annoyed to see the boy holding first a silver spoon and then a cup over the steam puffing out of the spout, and counting the number of drops into which the steam was condensed.

Watt's parents saw that the boy had a bent towards mechanics, and they encouraged it.

Watt the elder was a shipbuilder, engineer, shipchandler, and merchant at Greenock. In 1755, at the age of nineteen, James went to London to serve a year's apprenticeship under John Morgan of Finch Lane.

He returned to Scotland in the following year and attempted to open a business in Glasgow, but was barred because he lacked the privileges of a burgess of that city.

He obtained a position as mathematical instrument-maker to the University, and was provided with a shop within the college.

For six years he worked with indifferent success, but was popular at the University because of his versatility and his amiable character.

219

In 1763 he found a house in Glasgow and obtained a shop. At the same time he married.

For some years he did a variety of jobs—repairing organs and other musical instruments and inventing a number of curious but useful machines.

It was in 1759 that Watt began to occupy himself with the question of steam power.

Robison, a young professor at the University, conceived the idea that steam power might be applied to driving wheel-carriages, and suggested that a cylinder with its open end downward could be used to avoid using a working-beam.

Watt knew nothing of the steam engine at the time, but he began making a model with two cylinders of tin plate, intending that the pistons and the connecting-rods should act alternately on two pinions attached to the axles of the carriage-wheels.

The scheme was unsuccessful owing to defective construction. Watt therefore laid the idea aside.

Steam power had been discovered years before Watt's time. It was known 2000 years ago by the old Egyptian priests, who used it to cause images to move as if animated.

In the seventeenth century the Marquess of Worcester obtained some creditable effects with steam, though he was never successful in building a steam engine.

Three others—Savery, Papin, and Newcomen—carried experiments a little further. Watt began where Newcomen left off.

Learning that the University owned a model of the Newcomen steam engine, he suggested to his friend Dr Anderson, Professor of Natural Philosophy, that the model should be recovered from Sisson, an instrument-maker in London, with whom it had been left for repair.

Watt repaired the engine himself and, while experimenting, found that much of the steam was wasted, and that the condensation was imperfect.

After many experiments, Watt laid down a formula. He ascertained the expenditure of fuel in evaporating a given quantity of water, the quantity of cold water required to condense it again, and the relations between the temperature, pressure, and volume of the steam.

It was about the year 1765 that Watt appears to have finally met with success.

Robison relates that after his return to the University from a vacation in the country, he went to have a chat with Watt.

He found Watt sitting before the fire looking at a little tin cistern which he had on his knee.

Robison started his favourite conversation about steam, while Watt continued to look into the fire.

The young inventor was somewhat annoyed that Robison had communicated to a mechanic in the town a contrivance for turning the cocks of his engine, and when Robison pressed his question as to whether Watt had met with success, the latter replied : " You need not fash yourself any more about that, man. I have now made an engine that shall not waste a particle of steam. It shall all be boiling hot—ay, and hot water injected, if I please."

He pushed the little tin cistern with his foot under the table.

Watt would tell Robison no more.

On the same evening, Robison met a friend who also knew about Watt's experiments.

" Have you seen Jamie Watt ? " he asked.

" Yes. He'll be in fine spirits now with his engine."

" Yes," said Robison, " very fine spirits." Robison did not intend to show ignorance of the extent of Watt's experiments.

" Gad ! " returned the other, " the separate con-
denser's the thing. Keep it but cold enough, and you
may have a perfect vacuum, whatever be the heat of the
cylinder."

The nature of Watt's contrivance was clear to Robison
at once.

Robison was now concerned as to whether Watt
would give his invention away, but the inventor seemed
to have become cautious.

When Watt at last communicated the full results of
his experiments to Robison, the latter saw at once that
Watt had overcome his difficulties.

The question now was to market the invention.
This meant the construction of a model engine for
embodying the invention in a working form.

Watt hired an old cellar in King Street. He found it
easier to prepare the plan than to construct the model.
Nor could he find workmen capable of carrying out his
ideas.

Many difficulties had yet to be overcome. Defects
were found in the first model. Others had to be built.
In the end Watt was in a position to patent his device.

The specification of his patent taken out in 1769
read :

> The cylinder must, during the whole time the engine is
> at work, be kept as hot as the steam that enters it ; first, by
> inclosing it in a case of wood or any other materials that transmit
> heat slowly ; secondly, by surrounding it with steam or other
> heated bodies ; and, thirdly, by suffering neither water nor any
> other substance colder than the steam to enter or touch it during
> that time . . .
>
> Whatever air or other elastic vapour is not condensed by the
> cold of the condenser and may impede the working of the
> engine is to be drawn out by means of pumps . . .

There is another part of the specification which deals
with oils and lubricants for the piston instead of water.

The cost of obtaining this patent was defrayed by Dr John Roebuck in return for two-thirds of the profits.

Before any profit was made, Roebuck became financially involved, and was unable to carry on the enterprise.

In 1775, Roebuck's share in the patent was bought by Matthew Boulton, of Birmingham, who promoted the invention with energy.

He obtained an Act of Parliament for the extension of the terms of the patent, and he and Watt entered into partnership in Soho, where Watt took a house. Boulton supplied the capital. Watt managed the mechanical side.

They began to apply Watt's inventions to the pumping-engines of mines on the basis that they should receive one-third of the cost saved in fuel.

This scheme brought the partners a large sum of money. They continued to patent successive inventions until the steam engine was used for many other purposes.

In 1800, at the expiration of the term of the original patent, Watt and Boulton retired, and the business was handed over to their sons.

Watt was elected a Fellow of the Royal Society of Edinburgh in 1784, and of the Royal Society of London a year later. In 1806 he received the honorary degree of LL.D. from the University of Glasgow.

During a visit to France in 1786 he made the acquaintance of Berthollet, who taught him the use of chlorine for bleaching. On returning to England he handed the secret over to his father-in-law, Macgregor, who used it for the first time in Britain.

In 1808 he founded a prize for essays in natural philosophy to be competed for yearly at the University of Glasgow.

In 1816 he gave his native town, Greenock, a library and institute.

Sir Walter Scott said of him : "This potent commander of the elements . . . was one of the best and kindest of human beings."

Watt died on August 19, 1819, and was buried at Handsworth. A monumental statue by Chantrey was erected to his memory in Westminster Abbey.

XXXIX

LAFAYETTE, THE HERO OF TWO WORLDS

MARIE-JEAN-GILBERT MOTIER, Marquis of Lafayette, took part in three revolutions without rising to great eminence.

He was too honest. It was said of him that he left the keys in the locks, even in politics.

He took part in the American War of Independence, but there was a greater man there than Lafayette—George Washington.

Fate might have dealt him a better hand in France. Lafayette's revolutionary ideas, however, were pale pink. When the Reign of Terror began he was nauseated by the excesses of the mob. And the man who might have been the Cromwell of France disappeared like a pricked bubble.

Lafayette was born at the castle of Chavagnac in Auvergne on September 6, 1757, a short time after the death of his father at the battle of Minden. Educated at the College of Plessis in Paris, he married, at the age of sixteen, a daughter of the Duke of Ayen.

He served in the army, but when the British Colonies in America revolted, he was actuated by the desire to help in the overthrow of what he believed to be an oppressive British *régime*.

He was not the only Frenchman to offer his sword to the colonists ; but none made such great sacrifices for the cause of liberty.

Despite the prohibition of the King of France, the

opposition of his family, and the tears of his young wife, Lafayette fitted out a ship at his own expense, and in 1777 sailed for America.

The American Assembly was then sitting at Philadelphia. He offered his services as a volunteer, declaring that he would defray all his own expenses.

General Washington took a fancy to the young man. Lafayette had an honest enthusiasm which matched his own.

He was wounded at the battle of Brandywine, and was out of the fray for six weeks. He was in command of the Virginian division at Gloucester, but failed in an expedition to Canada in 1778.

He took part in the retreat at Barren Hill, was present at the battle of Monmouth, and Sullivan's withdrawal after the abortive attack on Rhode Island.

Lafayette left America when war broke out between England and France. Arriving home in February, 1779, he was received with favour by the Court, though he was nominally an outlaw for leaving France without permission.

The reputation of Lafayette had preceded him. He was fêted by every one, but when he began to ask for French assistance for the American colonists it was refused.

He conceived the idea of fitting out an expedition for raiding the English coast on behalf of the Americans, but his elaborate scheme fell through.

At length, however, 4000 men, under Count Rochambeau, were sent to America by the French Government. Lafayette himself returned to the United States in 1780, and was received with enthusiasm.

The surrender of Lord Cornwallis at Yorktown in 1781 was due mainly to the skill of Lafayette.

Lafayette returned to Europe soon afterwards, and

LAFAYETTE
Engraved from a portrait by Rasset

was about to organize an expedition against the British possessions when the peace with America was signed on September 3, 1783. Next year he paid his third visit to the United States, and was again received with demonstrations of gratitude.

Matters at home were now moving towards a revolution, and Lafayette, believing that a king was a " useless being," returned to France.

He sat in the Assembly of Notables in 1787 when the state of the Government's finances was being discussed. He advocated the setting up of a National Assembly. The words had an ominous sound ; they indicated revolution.

He had much to say about the liberty of the subject.

" Do you demand the convocation of the States-General ? " said the Count d'Artois.

" Yes, Prince, and even better than that," replied Lafayette.

" Write it down," said the Prince to the secretaries.

It was the beginning of the new history of France.

The Bastille had fallen. The citizens were organizing themselves into a military force. Who was to take command ? In the Town Hall stood the bust of Lafayette, presented by Virginia to the city of Paris. Dramatically, the President pointed to the bust. Lafayette was elected General of the National Guard with unanimity.

But Lafayette's revolutionary ideas could not keep pace with the unrestrained madness of the people. The Revolution had taken an unexpected course. He could not prevent the unnecessary executions. Lafayette resigned, and was only induced to resume his command after much pressure.

He rode about on his white horse vainly trying to preserve order. For a time he kept down the mob, but when, on October 6, the *citoyens* began their march on Versailles to bring back the King, he was unable to stand the torrent. His grenadiers revolted, and he was compelled to march with them.

Next day, when the mob furiously attacked the palace, he succeeded in mastering the crowd and saving the lives of the King and his family.

The King was brought to Paris, where Lafayette did his utmost to preserve Louis as a constitutional monarch.

Until the beginning of 1791, Lafayette was the leader of a perfectly constitutional revolution. In June of that year Danton demanded " the person of the King, or the head of the Commandant-general."

A month later an immense mob gathered for the purpose of signing a petition for the deposition of the King. Lafayette declared martial law and fired into the crowd. It was the beginning of the end of his popularity.

In October he resigned the command of the national guard and retired to his country seat.

Meanwhile he was very concerned at the proceedings in Paris. On June 28, 1792, he appeared before the Assembly to demand a change. They refused to listen to him. He was denounced by Robespierre before the Assembly, but a majority refused to carry the accusation.

After the fateful 10th of August, when Louis was taken a prisoner to the Assembly, Lafayette anticipated a decree of accusation by flying across the frontier.

He was captured by the Austrians, and was kept in various German prisons for five years. He was set at liberty on September 19, 1797, but he was not allowed to enter France until Napoleon became first consul. He was given the allowance of his military rank, but never received office. Napoleon, in fact, thought him a fool.

On the restoration of the Emperor, Lafayette returned

to Paris and was made Vice-president of the House of Representatives.

After the battle of Waterloo he took a prominent part in securing the abdication of the Emperor.

When Paris was occupied by the Allies, he again retired to his country seat, where he remained until 1817.

In 1824, Lafayette went to America, travelled through all the States of the Union, and was banqueted everywhere.

Congress voted him an estate in Virginia and a grant of 200,000 dollars for his services in the War of Independence.

Returning to France he found Charles X on the throne.

" I know but two men," said Charles, " who have always professed the same principles ; they are myself and M. Lafayette."

In 1830, Lafayette declared himself a leader in the new revolution. He was elected Commander of the National Guard, and assisted in choosing Louis Philippe king.

In June, 1832, he was once more nearly forced into the leadership of a revolution.

He died on May 20, 1834.

XL

The Bard of Caledonia

ROBERT BURNS was slowly dying.
"I fear it will be some time before I tune my lyre again," he said. "By Babel's streams I have sat and wept. I have only known existence by the pressure of sickness and counted time by the repercussions of pain. I close my eyes in misery and open them without hope."

Two months later, with the possibility of passing the remainder of his days in gaol, he wrote to his brother for the loan of £10 to preserve his freedom.

Thus does Fate reward the great.

Though "old and young, grave and gay, learned and ignorant were alike transported" with his poems, it was his simplicity and humility which withheld him from grasping the plums which might have been his.

Sir Walter Scott bears testimony to Robert's extraordinary independence :

> I was a lad of fifteen when he came to Edinburgh, but had sense enough to be interested in his poetry, and would have given the world to know him . . . I remember his shedding tears over a print representing a soldier lying dead in the snow, his dog sitting in misery on one side, on the other his widow with a child in her arms.
>
> His person was robust, his manners rustic, not clownish. His countenance was more massive than it looks in any of his portraits. There was a strong expression of shrewdness in his lineaments ; the eye alone indicated the poetic character and

temperament. It was large and of a dark cast, and literally glowed when he spoke with feeling or interest. I never saw such another eye in a human head.

He was much caressed in Edinburgh, but the efforts made for his relief were extremely trifling.

Though Burns contracted friendships with many of the great Scottish people, he preferred to share a bed in the garret of a writer's apprentice, for which they paid three shillings a week.

Burns was the son of William Burness, and was born in a cottage two miles from Ayr. The family were so poor that Burns was not able to receive even the cheap schooling of those days. He was threshing corn at the age of thirteen, and at fifteen was the chief labourer on his father's farm.

And so on to his thirtieth year, when his shoulders were bent, and the normally robust frame had become twisted by the years spent at the plough.

It was at this stage of his life that he was attacked by fits of melancholia which drove him to stimulants. Nevertheless, ambition was eating his soul, together with an overwhelming desire to get away from these hard tasks.

At meals he would sit with a spoon in one hand and a book in the other, and while in the fields he would pore over volumes of verse. Behind the plough he had plenty of time for thought, and the wish :

> That I for poor auld Scotland's sake
> Some useful plan or book could make,
> Or sing a sang at least,

would come perpetually to his mind.

His first verses of note, " Behind yon hills where Stinchar flows," were written about 1780 The following year he went to learn the trade of a flax-dresser.

Burns records that this was an " unlucky affair."
" As we were giving a welcome carousal to the New Year,
the shop took fire and burned to ashes ; and I was left
like a true poet, without a sixpence."

Then followed a blow to his affections, which he himself relates in a quaint way. He was studying mathematics till " the sun entered Virgo, when a charming
fillette, who lived next door, overset my trigonometry,
and set me off at a tangent from the scene of my studies."

The story is a sad one ; the poet was jilted, fell into
black despair, and had to resort to other means of con-
solation.

That Robert's shortcomings overshadowed his brilliance was evident. When he was twenty-five, his
father died, full of sorrow at young Burns's mode of
living.

After the old man's death, Robert and his brother
Gilbert remained at their farm at Lochlea, but neither
were keen farmers. In 1784 the family migrated to
Mossgiel, and for another four years Burns continued on
the farm earning less than a common labourer.

He then fell in love with his future wife, Jean Armour,
but her father refused to allow the marriage, and in 1786
Burns decided to seek solace abroad. He obtained a
situation as bookkeeper to a slave-estate in Jamaica, and
had actually booked his passage in a ship to the West
Indies, when his first volume, which was published in the
same year, brought him a sum of money.

The book, which included " The Twa Dogs," " The
Author's Prayer," " The Dream," " Hallowe'en," and
others, together with some of his most popular songs,
earned him about £20 and a literary reputation. At
Edinburgh he was feasted and admired, but through it
all maintained a stolid demeanour, refusing to be diverted
from his normal though exaggerated sense of humility.

This book was so greatly in demand that a friend of Burns wrote :

> I can well remember how even ploughboys and maid-servants would have gladly bestowed the wages they earned the most hardly, and which they wanted to purchase necessary clothing, if they might but procure the works of Burns.

In 1787 the second edition of the poems came out, and Burns received £400. On the strength of this success he took rambles through the Border towns into England as far as Newcastle, and a grand tour through the East Highlands, as far as Inverness, returning by Edinburgh and back to Ayrshire.

In 1788, Burns took another farm at Ellisland and married, but lost what little money he had left. Here he wrote, among others, " Auld Lang Syne " and " Tam o' Shanter."

His financial position at this time was deplorable, and it was only with difficulty that the Government were induced to grant him an appointment as excise officer in the district, which brought him £50 a year. A year or two later he took a similar position at Dumfries, worth £70 a year.

Next year he wrote about one hundred songs for George Thomson, to be incorporated in *Select Collection of Original Scottish Airs, with Symphonies and Accompaniments for the Pianoforte and Violin : the Poetry by Robert Burns.* Some of them were among the best Scottish songs ever written.

For this contribution Burns received a shawl for his wife, a picture by David Allan representing the " Cottar's Saturday Night," and £5.

He wrote a strong letter of protest, apparently without effect, and refused thereafter to write again for money.

Though his poems were popular, he was not. His

independent spirit repelled most people, and his revolutionary principles lost him much support.   In the last years of his life he was exiled from society, his temper became frayed, and he fell deeper into dissipation with people in the lower ranks of life, with whom he seemed to be more at home.

He was only thirty-seven when he died, a prematurely aged man.   For some time before his death he appears to have been a broken reed.   Once a friend invited him to a country ball, and he replied, " That's all over now," and recited a verse of Lady Grizel Baillie's ballad :

> O were we young as we ance hae been,
> We sud hae been galloping down on yon green,
> And linking it ower the lily-white lea,
> But were na my heart light I wad dee.

The funeral of Burns was reported in a newspaper at the time as follows :

> Actuated by the regard which is due to the shade of such a genius, his remains were interred on Monday last, the 25th July, with military honours, and every suitable respect.   The corpse having been previously conveyed to the town hall of Dumfries, remained there until the following ceremony took place : The military there, consisting of the Cinque Port Cavalry and the Angusshire Fencibles, having handsomely tendered their services, lined the streets on both sides of the burial-ground.
>
> The Royal Dumfries Volunteers, of which he was a member —in uniform, with crepe on their left arms, supported the bier ; a party of that corps, appointed to perform the military obsequies, moving in slow, solemn time to the " Dead March in Saul," which was played by the military band—preceded in mournful array with arms reversed.
>
> The principal parts of the inhabitants and neighbourhood, with a number of particular friends of the bard, from remote parts, followed in procession ; the great bells of the churches tolling at intervals.
>
> Arrived at the churchyard gate, the funeral party, according to the rules of that exercise, formed two lines and leaned their

heads on their firelocks, pointed to the ground. Through this
space the corpse was carried. The party drew up alongside the
grave and, after the interment, fired three volleys over it. The
whole ceremony presented a solemn, grand, and affecting
spectacle, and accorded with the general regret for the loss of a
man whose like we shall scarce see again.

Burns left a widow with five infant children and with
the hourly expectation of a sixth. His widow survived
him thirty-eight years, and died in the same room in
which he had died. Long after Burns was dead his
" bonnie Jean " was the object of much local interest, and
if her husband had succeeded in alienating society, she,
during the rest of her life, was a model of amiableness.
She was comely and good-looking even when approaching the age of sixty.

Burns has no place in Westminster Abbey, yet when
his anniversary comes round it is celebrated in every
country of the world. It is curious that he himself should
jocularly remark that his birthday would be celebrated
among other notable events.

In a letter to an early patron, Gavin Hamilton, in
1786, he writes :

> For my own affairs, I am in a fair way of becoming as
> eminent as Thomas à Kempis, or John Bunyan ; and you may
> expect henceforth to see my birthday inscribed among the
> wonderful events, in the Poor Robin and Aberdeen Almanacks,
> along with the Black Monday and the battle of Bothwell Bridge.

When he died he was unable to remunerate his
doctor, and he therefore asked the medical attendant to
accept his pair of pistols as a memento of their friendship.

Dr Maxwell ever afterwards proved a generous friend
to the widow and children, and retained the weapons until
his death in 1834, after which they were preserved by his
sister. They were then placed in Edinburgh Museum.

XLI

WILLIAM PITT, PREMIER AT TWENTY-FOUR

WHEN William Pitt the elder became Earl of Chatham, little William, who was then seven years of age, exclaimed : " I am glad that I am not the eldest son. I want to speak in the House of Commons like papa."

At fourteen the lad was a man in intellect, so that William Hayley, the author, who was introduced to him, was overawed by the wisdom expounded by Pitt, and regretted afterwards that he had not submitted one of his plays to the judgment of the boy, who had already written a tragedy with a political plot.

The rapid development of young Pitt caused considerable satisfaction to his parents, who were, however, distressed to notice that it was accompanied by an alarming growth physically.

He grew so quickly that they began to despair of being able to rear him. The boy was always weak and ill, and the only remedy that appeared efficacious was port wine, which young Pitt consumed in quantities that would have made drunk a full-grown man.

Such a regimen would have killed most boys, but Pitt thrived on it, for by the time that he was fifteen his health had considerably improved, although he was never strong.

Unlike his great contemporaries, North, Fox, Sheridan, Canning, Wellesley, and others, Pitt was never sent to a public school, although his father had himself been a distinguished Etonian.

The boy's health troubles made it necessary for him to be educated at home, and he was coached by a clergyman named Wilson

Nevertheless, before he was sixteen he had a remarkable knowledge of the ancient languages and mathematics.

In 1773 he went to Pembroke Hall, Cambridge, under Pretyman. The two became great friends, and within ten years the pupil had reached such eminence that he was able to make his preceptor Bishop of Lincoln.

At the University, Pitt avoided indulgence in pleasure. He never went to an evening party. At seventeen he was a Master of Arts, but he was deficient in many subjects which the average university graduate assimilated, particularly literature.

During one of the vacations he was introduced to Charles James Fox on the steps of the throne in the House of Lords. Fox was ten years older than Pitt, and already one of the keenest debaters England had ever possessed, but at this early stage Pitt was almost his equal.

Years afterwards Fox would relate the story of this meeting, and how the younger man had impressed him with his precocity.

On the death of his father, the Earl of Chatham, in May, 1778, young Pitt found it necessary to follow a profession. He left Cambridge, was called to the Bar, and took chambers at Lincoln's Inn.

He was then twenty-one, and when, in the autumn of that year there was a general election he offered himself as a candidate for the University. He was returned at the bottom of the poll, it being regarded as a presumption for a young man to stand for a university.

Soon he was a Member of Parliament for the borough of Appleby, through the patronage of Sir James Lowther. In February, 1781, he made his first speech in support of Edmund Burke's plan of economic reform.

Fox had already been on his feet, but he gave way to the young man. When Pitt, with his tall frame towering above his surroundings, began to speak, and Burke heard the silver tones of his voice and the perfect structure of his sentences, Burke exclaimed : " It is not a chip of the old block ; it is the block itself."

Another member remarked : " Pitt will be one of the first men in Parliament."

" He is so already," replied Fox.

Soon after this debate Pitt became a member of Brooks's on the proposal of Fox.

Three times during that session Pitt addressed the House, and during the prorogation acquitted himself with a number of briefs on the Western Circuit, being highly complimented by the judges.

In November, when Parliament resumed, Pitt spoke with brilliance in the debate on the Address. Then North's Government fell, and Rockingham became First Minister, with Fox and Shelburne Secretaries of State.

Pitt was offered the Vice-Treasurership of Ireland, an easy and highly paid post, but he declined without hesitation.

He wanted a seat in the Cabinet, and he intended to accept no post which did not carry this honour. Pitt supported Rockingham, but the Government was rent by conflicting opinions, and when, before it had existed three months, Rockingham died, the Duke of Portland was regarded as his successor.

This state of affairs did not suit Burke, Fox, and Lord John Cavendish, who immediately resigned. Pitt was offered the office of Chancellor of the Exchequer, and he accepted, while still only twenty-three.

Parliament met in December, 1782, and in the next February, when the American settlement was being debated, Pitt was not at his best. He even descended to cheap sarcasm, advising Sheridan to confine himself to amusing theatrical audiences, to which the dramatist retorted :

> After what I have seen and heard to-night, I really feel strongly tempted to venture on a competition with so great an artist as Ben Jonson and bring on the stage a second Angry Boy.

But Pitt was back in his old form a few days afterwards when the Opposition, a coalition between North and Fox, proposed a resolution censuring the treaties, but this did not prevent a minority vote, and Shelburne, the Prime Minister, resigned.

A reshuffle of parties left the Duke of Portland as First Lord of the Treasury, with Fox and North as Secretaries of State, after Pitt had been offered by George III the first place at the Treasury, which he repeatedly refused.

As the result of another political upheaval in the following year, Pitt became First Lord of the Treasury and Chancellor of the Exchequer. On the Opposition benches were Fox, Burke, North, and Sheridan, who made things uncomfortable for the young Prime Minister.

The country was almost solid for Pitt, and the City of London presented him with the freedom. He was feasted at Grocers' Hall, and the shopkeepers in the Strand and Fleet Street illuminated their houses in his honour.

On this evidence of the country's goodwill, Pitt refused to capitulate. Gradually the Opposition weakened, and in a debate in March the Government were beaten by only one vote.

Parliament was then suddenly dissolved, and Pitt went to the country, a hundred and sixty supporters of the coalition losing their seats. Pitt himself came in at the head of the poll for Cambridge University.

At the age of twenty-four Pitt ruled the Cabinet, and was the favourite of George III, of Parliament, and of the nation.

The eight years following the election of 1784 were prosperous for England. Then came a great change in the sentiments of Pitt.

The French Revolution, which he had approved at the outset, caused a violent reaction in the country, and he had to adjust his opinions with those of the people.

He worked hard to prevent the European War, and even when the guns were booming on the Continent he believed that England would not be drawn into it.

At last, pushed on by friends and opponents alike, he went to war, but prosecuted it with such laxity and half-heartedness that the English army, after an eight years' campaign, was the laughing-stock of Europe.

Despite his mistakes abroad, Pitt continued to rule the House of Commons until the Opposition had dropped to twenty-five.

Then followed a period of persecution, in which old laws which provided for severe punishment against political offenders were re-enacted. The Habeas Corpus Act was repeatedly suspended, and any public meeting fell under grave suspicion.

Many men of cultivated minds were sent to Botany Bay for uttering indiscreet phrases, and hundreds of reformers were indicted for treason.

This sudden change from tolerance to intolerance was one of the most remarkable incidents in the career of Pitt.

When he quarrelled with the King over the Irish

Union and Pitt's proposals for the emancipation of Roman Catholics, the Prime Minister resigned and went into retirement.

But the threat of invasion by Napoleon caused the King to entrust Pitt with the formation of a government, and he entered upon his second administration.

Disaster after disaster was occurring on the Continent. Nothing seemed able to stop Napoleon, and Pitt's difficulties at this time were so great that his health began to fail.

He retired to Bath, and while there he heard that a great battle had been lost in Moravia, that the coalition was dissolved, and that the Continent was at the mercy of France.

By slow journeys he came up from Bath to attend Parliament on January 21, 1806. He was carried into his bedroom at Putney, and there he met his friend the Marquess Wellesley, who had been Governor of India.

The excitement of the meeting was too much for him and he fainted away. Wellesley left the house convinced that the end had come.

He was unable to attend the meetings of the Commons, but still believed that he was in no danger until his old tutor, the Bishop of Lincoln, disillusioned him and spoke of spiritual matters.

Pitt died at a moment when the affairs of the country were in a deplorable state. Many stories are told of devout sentiments uttered by him in the last stages of his illness, but those who knew him best never credited them. Wilberforce declared that Pitt was a man who " always said less than he thought on such topics."

It was asserted that the dying man cried, " Oh, my country," and uttered many broken sentences about the state of public affairs.

He died on the morning of January 23, 1806, the

16

twenty-fifth anniversary of the day on which he took his first seat in Parliament. He was forty-six, and for nearly nineteen years had been First Lord of the Treasury.

When a resolution was introduced into the House of Commons that Pitt should be accorded a public funeral, it was carried by 288 votes to 89. Princes, nobles, bishops, and privy councillors attended, and Wilberforce, Pitt's greatest friend, carried the banner before the hearse.

Wilberforce declared afterwards that the " eagle of Chatham from above seemed to look down with consternation into the dark house which was receiving all that remained of so much power and glory."

Pitt left behind a debt of £40,000. How these debts were contracted, in view of the salary which he received while in office, was a mystery.

Nevertheless, the Government concurred in the payment of his debts.

Pitt, despite his popularity, was a most abused man. He was said to have been a strenuous opponent of parliamentary reform. Yet he himself introduced three motions for reform.

Protestants who fought against Roman Catholic emancipation would declare themselves to be Pittites, although Pitt had resigned his office through his proposals for relieving Roman Catholics.

Pitt was a free trader, yet the most ardent anti-free traders called themselves Pittites.

There was therefore a mythical Pitt as well as a genuine Pitt as widely apart as the poles in principle.

Pitt was never a patron of the arts. He believed that poetry, literature, painting, and sculpture were to be endured rather than praised.

It was customary for authors, poets, artists, sculptors, and architects to receive some recompense from the State, but Pitt would grant nothing to these people even though they heaped praises upon him. He may have been right in his opinion that art should be a marketable quantity, and his apathy did tend to remove for a time the abuses that had been going on for many years. There were, in those days, talented men without life's necessaries, who deserved help from the State.

Samuel Johnson's *English Dictionary* and *Lives of the Poets* made no impression on Pitt. When a stay in a warmer climate would have enabled Johnson to live a year or two longer, no help could be obtained from the First Lord of the Treasury.

Even sculptors, who had been commissioned by Parliament to execute monuments, appealed to the Treasury for years and eventually had to petition the King before they could secure the payments to which they were entitled.

XLII

The Lowly Grave of Sir John Moore

Slowly and sadly we laid him down,
   From the field of his fame fresh and gory ;
We carved not a line and we raised not a stone—
   But we left him alone in his glory.

AN hour before dawn on the morning of January 17,
1809, a handful of soldiers began turning over the
earth with their bayonets on the ramparts of Corunna.
They were digging the grave of Sir John Moore, hero of
Corunna.

The Rev. Charles Wolfe, in his poem, relates that
" Not a soldier discharged his farewell shot " over
the grave. It was the dead man's wish that no fuss
should be made. There was no coffin—not even a
shroud.

Early the day before, Sir John Moore had received
a mortal wound in the battle which saved Spain from
Napoleon. When his men made to unbuckle his belt
as he lay on the ground, he waved them away, though the
hilt of his sword was pressing into the wound.

As his life was slowly ebbing, he insisted on dictating
a report commending to the Government the names of
those who had fought so well and distinguished themselves
in the battle. He died with the name of Lady Hester
Stanhope on his lips.

There was as much controversy about the battle of
Corunna as about any battle in the history of England.
The Peninsular War was a thing of the past before the

events of the campaign were examined without political bias, and the true facts brought to light.

Following a bold thrust at the French line of communications which had diverted Napoleon from his projected advance against Lisbon and Andalusia, Moore, with 25,000 men, began on Christmas Day, 1808, a retreat on to his new base at Corunna. Behind him was Napoleon with 70,000 men, his advance guard of cavalry pressing closely on the heels of the English army.

Moore had just time to blow up the bridges of the Esla, but when he reached Astorga he found the inhabitants demoralized. It was impossible to billet his troops satisfactorily.

The issue of supplies was disorganized, and Moore's troops, tired of marching and countermarching, hungry and without discipline, broke open the wine stores. Soon many of them were drunk.

A round-up of the drunkards was carried out with difficulty, and throughout the retreat these men were shepherded along like sheep in front of Paget's Reserve Division, which, in addition, had to fight rearguard actions from time to time.

On January 1, Napoleon, thinking that Moore had eluded his clutches, handed the command over to Marshal Soult and returned to Paris. For days the English army marched westward with the French close behind, the English gradually becoming depleted through loss of men by sickness and capture. With the object of reviving the morale of his troops, Moore made a stand at Lugo. Instantly his men brightened up, but when Soult refused to attack, discipline became worse than ever.

Many officers and men were marching barefoot along the jagged mountain roads ; many died. There were frequent desertions ; bands of men broke ranks and wandered into the mountains plundering houses for food.

On January 11 Moore reached Corunna to find, with keen disappointment, that the fleet he expected had not arrived. A few ships were in the harbour, and, after transferring his sick men, Moore prepared for the coming battle with the 15,000 men now left of his army.

Three days later Soult arrived, and on the 16th he began the attack with 16,000 men and 20 guns. Moore was wounded at a moment when the tide of battle was going in favour of the English, his arm being shot off. The command devolved on Hope, who failed to follow up the advantage that had been gained. With nightfall the fighting stopped, but the British were able to embark on the ships of the fleet which arrived next day.

Over the grave of Moore, Marshal Soult directed that a monument should be erected, and in 1811 the temporary structure was made permanent at the instance of the Prince Regent.

On February 1 the Duke of York issued to the army an order which spoke of the fact that " the life of Sir John Moore was spent among the troops."

The situation between Sir John Moore and Lady Hester Stanhope is not exactly known. The two were very friendly, but there is no corroboration of the suggestion that they were betrothed. Moore did, however, form an attachment for Caroline Fox, afterwards the wife of Sir William Napier, but did not offer marriage because he feared to influence her through his friendship for her father " to an irretrievable error for her own future contentment."

Moore was born on November 13, 1761, and was the son of John Moore of Glasgow.

As a boy he was keen to become a soldier. When very young he was placed in the care of a clergyman in Switzerland to master the French and German languages.

At the age of fifteen he joined the 51st Regiment, in which he was appointed ensign. About this time, however, his father, who was a doctor, was chosen by the Duchess of Hamilton as a tutor for her son. The young duke was of delicate constitution, and required the care of a physician.

The young Moore was a handsome youth, of elegant and graceful manners. When the Duchess saw him, she was so pleased with his accompaniments that she asked that he might accompany his father and the family on their journeys on the Continent.

Moore and the son of the Duchess were about the same age, and, both being attractive young men, they attracted the attention of distinguished people on the Continent.

The Emperor Joseph made Moore an offer if he would quit the English army and enter the Austrian service, but he respectfully refused.

At the end of the tour he joined the 82nd Regiment, to which in the meantime he had been promoted lieutenant.

In four years Moore was a captain, and paymaster to the regiment.

Having very little knowledge of accounts, and finding himself in difficulties, he asked for leave of absence and went to Glasgow, where he entered the counting-house of a merchant as a clerk. When he returned to his regiment he knew all there was to be known about accounts.

His regiment was sent to America for the American War. When it was disbanded in 1783, Moore returned to England and became member of Parliament for the united boroughs of Lanark, Peebles, and Linlithgow.

He was no more than an ornament in the House of Commons, for he never opened his mouth, although he held the seat for six years.

In the meantime, however, he became a close friend of Pitt and Burke, and also of the Duke of York.

In 1790 he joined his battalion in Ireland, and almost immediately was sent to Corsica, where he was engaged to assist General Paoli in driving out the French.

The French were forced to leave the island, and Moore was left to guard it in case of a second invasion. When a disagreement arose between Moore and the English Governor he was recalled.

In addition to the French, Corsica was in danger from the bands of brigands which infested the mountains. Time and again they made raids on the plantations, plundered them, and kept the inhabitants in a state of constant alarm.

Moore pursued them into the wildest recesses of the mountain, and caused them—one band after the other— to surrender.

Sickness prevailed among the troops, and two-thirds of Moore's army died in one year. Moore himself shared the tribulations of the troops. He lived like the rest on salt pork and biscuits, and at night slept in the woods with no covering but his cloak.

Moore at last fell sick, and though his medical attendants advised him to leave the country, he refused until he became unconscious. He was carried to a ship, but after a little time at sea he recovered.

It is said that Moore was recalled from Corsica because of his friendship with certain Corsican patriots.

Later, Moore was present at the battle of Aboukir during the Egyptian campaign, and was wounded by a musket ball. During his convalescence the French surrendered at Cairo, and Moore was instructed to see the French army off the premises. He had only six thousand men, while the French had eleven thousand. The two armies marched side by side, the French still being fully

armed.   At any moment the French might have turned
on Moore and overwhelmed him.

On taking leave of Moore, the French Commander
explained : " General Moore, never was a more orderly
and better regulated movement executed than has been
performed by your troops ! "

In 1798 Moore went to Ireland as Major-general,
and was in command of a corps during the rebellion.
Defeating a large force of Irish, he saved Wexford from
destruction.   A year later he appointed to command a
brigade in the Dutch expedition, and was wounded.

Soon afterwards he was made Colonel of the 52nd
Regiment.

Pitt made Moore a Knight of the Bath, and at about
the same time he was promoted to Lieutenant-general.

XLIII

GEORGE STEPHENSON, " ENGINE-DOCTOR "

A T the opening of the Liverpool and Manchester
Railway on September 15, 1830, the Right Hon.
William Huskisson, ex-President of the Board of Trade,
was killed.

According to newspaper reports there were present
at this affair " upwards of 1000 gentlemen," including the
Duke of Wellington, then head of the Government.

Those composing the party were in thirty carriages,
drawn by eight of the engines of George Stephenson.

The trains were decorated with coloured streamers
" and all the paraphernalia of joyousness and delight."

One engine, the *Northumbrian*, with three carriages,
was on one set of rails, while other engines and carriages
were on a second set of rails.

In the three carriages hauled by the *Northumbrian*
were the band, the Duke of Wellington, Prince Esterhazy,
Sir Robert Peel, Mr Huskisson, and the directors of the
railway.

Wellington's carriage was 32 feet long and 8 feet wide.
It had a canopy 24 feet long, supported by gilded pillars.
The drapery was of rich crimson cloth, and on top was a
ducal coronet.

When the train arrived at Newton it was found necessary to take in water, and during the delay, Huskisson
got down from his carriage and went to pay his respects
to the Duke.

Huskisson had held office in the Duke's ministry, but

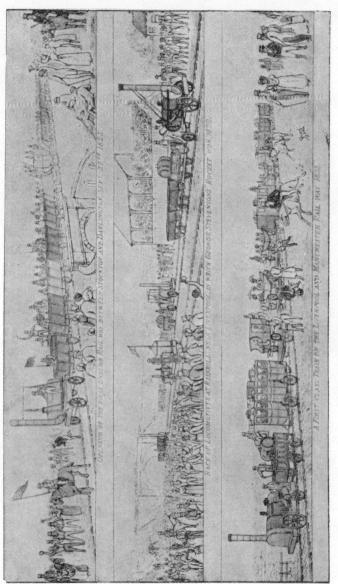

OPENING OF THE FIRST ENGLISH RAILWAY BETWEEN STOCKTON AND DARLINGTON, SEPT. 27TH 1825

RACE OF LOCOMOTIVES AT RAINHILL, NEAR LIVERPOOL, WHICH GEORGE STEVENSONS' ROCKET WON, 1829

A FIRST CLASS TRAIN ON THE LIVERPOOL AND MANCHESTER RAIL WAY, 1833

SOME LANDMARKS IN RAILWAY HISTORY

in a petulant fit had resigned.   There is reason to believe that Huskisson intended to make his peace with the fiery Duke.

He had barely shaken hands with Wellington, when there were cries of " Get in I "

It was then seen that another engine was approaching on the other line.   In a panic, Huskisson ran up the ladder, and gripped the handle of the door.

But the door flew open, and Huskisson was swung from the steps and thrown into the path of the approaching train.

The engine that crushed Huskisson beneath its wheels was Stephenson's *Rocket* !

" The unfortunate gentleman shrieked dreadfully," says the newspaper report.

The ex-President of the Board of Trade was taken several miles along the line to the home of the Rev. Mr Blackburne, vicar of Eccles, and an engine was sent for doctors.

Preparations were then made for the cavalcade to go on, but the Duke refused to take any further part.

An argument ensued between the directors and Wellington, but the Duke could not be induced to continue with the plans.   He said that he was too upset at the death of his old colleague.

The civic fathers of Manchester and Salford then came forward, and added their persuasions.   If he did not go with the train, they argued, " the peace of their towns would be broken."

Whereupon the Duke gave way, and " the carriages came to their destination in gallant style."

The newspaper correspondent, in his quaint phraseology, continues :

> Along the road there was frequent hooting from the workmen who are opposed to this great national improvement, and

on more than one occasion stones were hurled at the carriages when passing along.

Considerable anxiety for the public peace was felt by many persons, there being such masses of people about, and not guided I regret to say, by the most peaceful and orderly spirit.

The garrison was under arms, and at various points within sight of the railway picquets of cavalry were placed.

Without this display of military force there would certainly have been a breach of the peace, the populace having taken determined possession of many parts of the railway, and in some evinced a bold and daring anxiety to tear it up.

Thus has opened this great national undertaking which is to shorten distances and facilitate communication in a manner which a few years back it had not entered into the mind of man even to conceive.

If a tragedy did mar the proceedings, the whole ceremony was nevertheless a great tribute to George Stephenson, who had risen from a cowherd to one of the greatest mechanical geniuses of his time in the course of half a century.

He was the father of the modern railway system, and was really the presiding genius of the Liverpool and Manchester Railway, which afterwards blossomed out into the London and North Western Railway.

George was born at Wylam, about eight miles west of Newcastle-on-Tyne, on June 9, 1781. He was the second of six children of Robert Stephenson, then fireman of a pumping engine at Wylam Colliery.

He was never educated in his childhood, and was employed successively as cowherd, ploughboy, and a driver of gin-horses.

He early showed a taste for engineering, and used to model in clay the steam-engines which he saw in the neighbourhood.

At the age of fourteen he was engaged to assist his father, then a fireman at Dewley. At fifteen he himself was employed as a fireman, and two years later he became a ' plugman ' in charge of the pumping apparatus of an engine.

At twenty he was promoted to ' brakesman,' and was noted at this age for his strength and activity.

He was also a competent shoemaker, could cut out clothes, and clean and mend clocks, and in his spare time he earned money at all these occupations.

He soon obtained much practical knowledge of steam-engines. But he lacked book-knowledge. He became aware of this discrepancy at the age of eighteen, and forthwith began to learn reading, writing, and arithmetic, by attending classes after working hours.

In 1802 he was appointed to look after the winding steam-engine of the inclined plane at Willington Quay on the Tyne, and on November 28 of that year he married Frances Henderson.

On October 16 of next year his son Robert was born, but in 1804 he lost his wife.

When his father lost his eyesight he was dependent on George for support, and after securing two or three situations, each subsequent one being better paid, George was drawn by ballot for the militia, the whole of his savings were swallowed up in finding a substitute.

He thought of emigrating to the United States, but had no money.

In 1810 he offered to repair a pumping-engine at Killingworth pit, and succeeded so well that he became known as the " engine-doctor."

His appointment as principal mechanical engineer of the colliery followed as a matter of course.

It was about the year 1812 that he turned his attention to the locomotive engine, which had already been in use on mineral railways.

The first practical locomotive was that of Trevithick, the Cornishman, but it was a cumbersome affair of rackwork rails, toothed driving-wheels, warping chains, and other gadgets.

It was discovered that all these contrivances were unnecessary. Smooth wheels would run on smooth rails without them.

About this time the proprietors of the Killingworth Colliery instructed Stephenson to build a locomotive.

It was tried in July, 1814, and was the first engine to run upon edge-rails.

In a second locomotive he introduced many improvements, and in 1823, with borrowed capital, he founded his engine factory. In 1829 he was able to obtain a greatly increased volume of steam.

On October 6, 1829, there was a great competition of locomotive engines for a prize offered by the directors of the Liverpool and Manchester Railway. It was gained by George Stephenson's *Rocket*, the parent of all present-day locomotives.

The *Rocket* was able to travel at thirty miles an hour, whereas ten miles an hour had been the previous limit.

Stephenson and his son, Robert, continued to build heavier and more powerful engines.

The eight engines used at the opening of the railway were driven by George himself, his son Robert, and his brother Robert.

George took a leading part in the subsequent extension of the various railway systems. He was the first engineer of the Grand Junction Railway connecting the Liverpool and Manchester with Birmingham, and in conjunction with his son, was chief engineer of the London and Birmingham Railway. He was also chief engineer of the Manchester and Leeds, the Birmingham and Derby, the Sheffield and Rotherham, the Midland, the York and North Midland, the Chester and Crewe, the Chester and Birkenhead, the Manchester and Birmingham, and the Maryport and Carlisle Railways, opened in 1839 and 1840.

Much money was lost in wild-cat railway schemes at the time, but Stephenson himself would have nothing to do with the financial side of any hare-brained promotion.

During the later years of his life he was connected with coal-mines and lime-works.

He had married his second wife, Elizabeth Hindmarsh, in 1819, and he lived in his affluent days with her at a large house near Chesterfield in the neighbourhood of his coal-mines.

George was generous to those in need, and during his early days in the mines he often faced the most terrible danger in endeavouring to rescue his fellow-workmen.

He died at the age of sixty-seven on August 12, 1848.

XLIV

Sir John Franklin, Polar Hero

ON March 13, 1854, the British Admiralty, following an inquiry, decided to strike off the Navy List the names of Sir John Franklin and his officers and crew.

Nothing had been heard of them since July, 1845, a short time after Franklin, with the ships *Erebus* and *Terror*, had sailed from Disco, on the west coast of Greenland.

At the end of July the two ships were sighted and spoken by a whaler in Melville Bay, while they were anchored to an iceberg. The crew appeared well and in good spirits, and on October 27, 1845, the news was published in London that all was well with the expedition.

Year after year passed away without any news of the explorers, and the Admiralty were at last reluctantly compelled to assume that the men had all perished.

What was the fate of the *Erebus* and *Terror* ? To this day it has never been cleared up, although within recent years fragmentary clues have been found, and theories have been advanced as to the last days of the expedition.

In 1930 new light was thrown on the matter by a survey following the story of a Nova Scotian captain, Peter Bayne, that Eskimos knew of certain vaults in which the remains of Sir John Franklin had been buried on King William Island, with his log and other papers.

Although the expedition to test the truth of the story came to nothing, there remained a belief in the Eskimo story.

It was also said that a sunken ship, presumably the *Erebus*, had been located.

The theory accepted as to the fate of the voyagers is that 105 men left the *Erebus* and *Terror*, which had been trapped in the ice for about twelve months.

They made their way down towards the mainland, most of them dying on the way. The graves of these men were eventually found after an aeroplane flight over the area.

There is evidence that some of the men died from scurvy, while others starved to death. As they dropped out from the main body, they were buried one by one by their comrades.

The bodies had been covered by cairns of stones, in one of which was found a blue jacket and tent coverings.

During the aeroplane flight the remains of a ship were also seen, but whether this was either of Franklin's vessels could not be established.

Early in 1934, speculation as to the fate of the expedition was revived by the discovery of a faded old document in an air-tight canister on the shore near Kirkcudbright, Scotland.

The document was an official form issued to ships of the Navy, and was printed in London in 1859, five years after the expedition had been adjudged lost.

It was believed to be an exact copy of the record of Franklin's quest for the North-West Passage which was found under a cairn at Point Victory, on the north-west coast of King William Land, by the *Fox* expedition, and brought to England in 1859.

After stating that the ships had wintered in the ice during 1846–7, it concluded with the information that all was well.

Then at the bottom of the sheet in the same handwriting was the message : " Party, consisting of two

17

officers and six men, left the ships on Monday, May 24,
1847."

Scribbled around the edge of the paper was the
information that the *Erebus* and *Terror* were deserted on
April 22, the officers and crews consisting of " 105 souls."
It was added that Sir John Franklin died on June 11,
1847, when the total loss of men to that date was 9 officers
and 15 men.

The original of this document was brought home by
Capt. (afterwards Admiral Sir) F. Leopold McClintock,
who commanded the *Fox* expedition.

How the copy came into existence is a mystery, but
it would appear that an exact copy of the original had
been made by some one on a similar form, and placed in
the canister which was found on the shores of the Dee.

The *Fox* expedition was sent out in 1859 by Lady
Franklin, the wife of the explorer, and they discovered
many relics. Following their investigations, a rather
elaborate and detailed theory as to what had occurred
was constructed.

According to this theory, the ships spent the winter of
1846–7 and 1847–8, in the ice near King William Land.
In April 1848 they left the ships and took with them two
whaleboats mounted on runners, with a large quantity of
articles and provisions.

In 1847 Franklin had died, and Captain Crozier, of
the *Terror*, had succeeded as commander.

Reaching Point Victory, Crozier wrote his last message
to the outer world, and the party then started south.
Subsequently, the party broke up into two portions, one
going on with one boat and the others deciding to return
to the ships, for some reason which will never be known.

Among the party going south was, it is believed,
Crozier, and certain remains indicate that they reached
the Great Fish River.

Nothing is known of what took place subsequently or how the men met their deaths.

During the years 1921 to 1924 Dr Knud Rasmussen, the Danish explorer, discovered further relics of the expedition. Others were found in 1926 by a trader ten miles across Simpson Strait from King William Land.

Major L. T. Burwash, of the North-West Territories and Yukon Branch Department of the Interior, Canada, was the commander of the aeroplane which made other finds in 1930.

With the one exception no logs or records of the Franklin expedition have been located.

According to statements made by Eskimos in 1859, one of the two ships drifted ashore, while the other sank in the ice, but this story was not considered reliable.

In 1851 two ships answering to the description of the *Erebus* and *Terror* were seen near the Newfoundland Banks by the brig *Renovation* while on a passage from Bristol to Quebec. Their appearance suggested that they had been deliberately abandoned.

When this news became public in 1852 the Admiralty held an inquiry, but were unable to come to any conclusion. It was held that it was unlikely that the ships could have drifted so far away from their base.

In 1932 a curious story came from Edmonton, Alberta. It was a suggestion by Napoleon Verville, the explorer, who had spent seven years in the Arctic, that certain Eskimos on Banks Land and Melville Island were descendants of members of the Franklin expedition.

Verville declared that he had spent five months with the Eskimos on Banks Lands, north of the Canadian mainland, and found that they had " milk-white skins except where their faces and hands had become tanned and weather-beaten."

He added :

> I am almost sure that they are sons or grandsons of members
> of the Franklin expedition. They told me, too, they had found
> skulls and bones of white men washed up along the coast from
> Prince of Wales Island down to the Boothia Peninsula.

Sir John Franklin was born at Spilsby, Lincolnshire,
on April 16, 1786. He was educated at St Ives and
Louth Grammar School, and his father was anxious that
he should enter the Church.

John had other ideas, and after a good deal of persuasion his father agreed that he should go to sea.

The story is told of young John that every half-holiday
he would walk twelve miles to see the ocean. He was
entered as midshipman on board the *Polyphemus* at the
age of fourteen, and served in the Baltic through the
battle of Copenhagen.

Returning to England, he was appointed to the
Investigator, which was commissioned for a voyage of
discovery to Australia.

During this voyage he had great opportunities for
scientific research. After two years the *Investigator* became unfit for further service and had to be abandoned,
the officers and men being taken on board the *Porpoise*,
which was on its way to England.

The *Porpoise* and her consort, the *Cato*, were wrecked
on a coral reef on the Australian coast, and while the
captain went in an open boat to Port Jackson, 250
leagues distant, Franklin and 94 others spent nearly
two months on the reef.

Franklin eventually arrived at Canton, and sailed
for Europe in the *Earl Camden*.

On arriving in England Franklin was appointed to
the *Bellerophon*, and was signal-midshipman during the
battle of Trafalgar. As lieutenant he served for six years

in the *Bedford*, was present at the blockade of Flushing, and at the disastrous attack on New Orleans.

Peace being restored, Franklin sought excitement in other directions, and he obtained an appointment in an expedition to the Polar Sea.

In June, 1819, he was placed in command of his first overland expedition, being instructed to proceed through Rupert's Land and trace the coast line of the North American continent.

During this expedition Franklin and his companions walked 5560 miles, and encountered privations of the most severe character. On his return to England he was made a commander and elected to the Royal Society.

In 1823 he married Eleanor, youngest daughter of William Porden.

In 1825 he went on his second land expedition, and traced the North American coast from the Coppermine River nearly to the 105th meridian. For a time he was in command of the *Rainbow* in the Mediterranean.

Then his wife died, and he married again.

He was appointed Governor of Antigua, and then of Van Dieman's Land. He returned to England in 1844, at a time when it was decided that a further expedition should be made to discover the North-West Passage.

Franklin applied for the job as commander. Lord Hatherton, who was head of the Admiralty, said : " Why, Sir John, I am told you are sixty years of age."

" No, no, my lord," replied Franklin, " only fifty-nine."

XLV

MICHAEL FARADAY, INVENTOR AND SANDEMANIAN

WHEN Michael Faraday, the inventor, was buried in Highgate Cemetery in August, 1867, there was no service.

Not a prayer was said, not a hymn sung.

It was not because Faraday had outraged the laws of society. Many famous people were present, including professors and scientists of the universities, to pay a last tribute to a man who had done much for chemistry.

The absence of a service was due to the fact that Faraday belonged to a strange religious sect known as the Sandemanians, or Glasites.

This school of religious thought was founded by John Glas, who taught that all Church establishments were unscriptural, and that each congregation should be self-governing and have the power to appoint its own ministers.

The publication of his views led to his suspension by the synod of Angus, and in 1730 he was deposed from the ministry.

His teachings, however, survived and were actually adopted by many intelligent people. Faraday, a deeply religious man, was one of the apostles of Sandeman, the teacher who carried on the ministry of the sect after the death of Glas.

One of the chief tenets of the community was " that the bare death of Jesus Christ without a thought or deed on the part of man is sufficient to present the chief of sinners spotless before God."

Michael Faraday was the son of a blacksmith, and was born on September 22, 1791. Michael did not like his father's trade, and the elder Faraday, believing that his son was destined for something better, apprenticed him to a bookbinder named Ribeau.

From the age of nine to twenty-one Faraday continued working among the books. There was ample time for study, and when a book was brought to him to bind he lost no opportunity of devouring its contents.

He might have been a bookbinder to the end of his life but for one of those curious pieces of fortune which have often started great men up the rung of the ladder.

It is recorded that one day Ned Magrath, formerly secretary to the Athenæum Club, walked into Ribeau's shop. There he saw " one of the bucks of the paper bonnet zealously studying a book he ought to have been binding."

He took a peep at the book, and he found that it was an encyclopædia. It was open at the section, " Electricity."

Magrath got into conversation with the workman, who, of course, was Faraday, and found that he had a knowledge of chemistry that was as extensive—and probably more so—than that of a professor.

Magrath gave Faraday some tickets for a course of lectures by Sir Humphry Davy at the Royal Institution.

Each day thereafter Faraday was to be seen perched, " pen in hand and his eyes starting out of his head, just over the clock opposite the chair."

At the end of the course Faraday sent to Davy brief particulars of himself.

Faraday himself records what happened :

> I took notes and afterwards wrote them out more fairly in a quarto volume. My desire to escape from trade, which I thought vicious and selfish, and to enter the service of science, which I imagined made its pursuers amiable and liberal, induced me at last to take the bold step of writing to Sir Humphry Davy, expressing my wishes and a hope that, if an opportunity came in his way, he would favour my views.
>
> At the same time I sent the notes I had taken of his lectures.

There was a remarkable sequel. Davy was about to start for a holiday, but had time to consider his correspondent's notes. He realized at once that Faraday had an exceptional grip on his subject.

Faraday's good fairy appeared suddenly one evening in the person of a messenger from Sir Humphry Davy himself.

Faraday was about to get into his humble bed, when there was a sound of wheels at the door.

He went to a window and saw a splendid equipage. A minute or two later a servant in livery handed the apprentice a note, asking him to call and see the great man next morning.

At the interview, Davy said that there were many obstacles in the way of a scientific career, but if the young man were determined, he would engage him as assistant at twenty-five shillings a week.

Faraday was overjoyed, and Davy himself never regretted taking the youth into his employ.

Years later, when Davy was congratulated on his great discoveries, he remarked, " My best discovery was Michael Faraday."

Faraday soon began to assist his patron in his lectures and in the laboratory. Then, when Davy went abroad, Faraday was promoted to the position of secretary and valet.

It is very difficult to understand the attitude of Lady Davy, Sir Humphry's wife. It is recorded that she did her utmost to show off the young man in the worst light. She emphasized continually the fact that he was only a menial under an obligation to her husband.

She insisted that Faraday should take his meals with the grooms.

The young man made no complaint, and when he returned to London he dived still further into undeveloped aspects of science.

He made a number of important discoveries in chemistry in conjunction with Sir Humphry Davy, and in 1827 he succeeded his master when he retired from the Royal Institution.

Faraday was offered many valuable posts in commercial undertakings, but he refused them all. In fact, it may be said that he never thought of himself or of monetary gain.

While Faraday's earlier researches concerned chemistry alone, he always had a desire to experiment in electricity. He succeeded in liquefying several gases, and produced new kinds of glass for optical purposes.

In 1821 he appears to have begun researches in electricity. After a number of minor discoveries, he attempted to obtain an electric current by means of a magnet, and to produce a current in one wire by means of a current in another wire, or by a magnet.

In 1831 he discovered that this could be done. To a friend named Phillips, he wrote :

I am busy just now again on electro-magnetism, and I think I have got hold of a good thing, but can't say. It may be a weed instead of a fish that, after all my labour, I may at last pull up.

A fortnight later he found that he had achieved success and had discovered the induction of electrical currents.

The first period of Faraday's electrical researches lasted ten years. In 1841 he read his paper, "Experimental Researches," to the Royal Society, and then decided to take a rest.

In 1845 he began to experiment again, and made discoveries on the effect of magnetism on polarized light. These were all published from time to time in the *Transactions* of the Royal Society.

Faraday refused the Presidency of the Royal Society and that of the Royal Institution. The only distinction that he would take was D.C.L., and at first he even declined a pension which Lord Melbourne, the Premier, offered him.

Perhaps his refusal had something to do with the way in which the pension was offered him. In those days a scientist was not held in very high esteem by a society which was as disreputable as it was ignorant.

Later, however, Melbourne realized that he had been dealing with a really great man, and he handsomely apologized.

In the end Melbourne made it easy for Faraday to accept a Civil List pension of £300 a year, to which was added later the tenancy of a house at Hampton Court.

At the age of thirty Faraday had married a charming woman who helped and encouraged him in his experiments. She it was who first saw his successful experiment in causing the magnetic needle to revolve round an electric current.

Faraday was careful to keep a list of his experiments. They were numerous. The last is numbered 16,041 !

From the researches of Faraday came the electric telegraph and telephone, and the many applications of electricity which has become such a boon in these days.

He was also a pioneer in the production of steel alloys ; while his experiments in chlorine, made when he was still in the employ of Davy, have enriched the textile industry.

In optics he was responsible for improvements in the manufacture of glass and the illumination of lighthouses, while even photography came out of his investigation of the vaporization of mercury.

Some of his lectures are keenly studied to-day, such as those on the chemistry of a candle.

Among his discoveries was benzine. This he announced to the Royal Society in 1825.

Faraday would never engage in controversy. He merely stated facts and let them stand on their own merits. He was free from pride and obtrusiveness. When he found that he was too old to concentrate on scientific work, he gave it up without complaint.

As a religious man he was sometimes criticized for his experiments. He replied to these criticisms in a lecture on mental education delivered in 1854 :

> High as man is placed above the creatures around him, there is a higher and far more exalted position within his view ; and the ways are infinite in which he occupies his thoughts about the fears, or hopes, or expectations of a future life.
>
> I believe that the truth of that future cannot be brought to his knowledge by any exertion of his mental powers, however exalted they may be ; that it is made known to him by other teaching than his own, and is received through simple belief of the testimony given.

His biographer, Dr Bence Jones, says of Faraday :

> His standard of duty was supernatural. . . . It was formed entirely on what he held to be the revelation of the will of God in the written word, and throughout all his life his faith led him to act up to the very letter of it.

Faraday died at Hampton Court on August 25, 1867.

XLVI

John Henry Newman goes over to Rome

ONE of the most dramatic incidents which followed the passing of the Catholic Emancipation Bill in 1829 was the appearance of John Henry Newman at a dinner in grey trousers.

To the lay observer this might mean nothing, but to his friends, who knew how punctilious he was in regard to wearing clerical garb, it indicated much.

For years Newman had been examining his position in relation to the Church of England. For months he had said nothing to his friends, although they knew that he was gradually drifting towards Rome. Many times they had discussed whether he would ultimately go a little further than his already advanced Anglo-Catholicism, and take the plunge.

Bernard Smith, Fellow of Magdalen, and Vicar of Leadenham, had submitted to Dr Nicholas Wiseman, the Pope's English representative, and afterwards Archbishop of Westminster. Many other Anglo-Catholics were wavering and showing a disposition to do the same, when Wiseman suggested that Smith should call upon Newman and get him to make the declaration.

Strangely enough, Newman had already been charged by the Bishop of Lincoln with inducing Smith to change his creed. Actually there was no truth in this, for Newman had all along adopted a passive attitude, and pleaded with Smith to see him before he made a decision.

Smith had given no heed, but when he went to Newman's house at the suggestion of Wiseman, he was received very cordially. Newman and a number of his friends who held the same views were living in cottages at Littlemore, Oxford, subsisting on two meals a day and preserving a complete silence for half a day.

To this community Smith went. In the evening Newman invited Smith to dinner with himself and his friends, and it was then that Newman appeared in grey trousers.

Smith, who had been Newman's curate at Littlemore, could not fail to understand the sign.

Denis Gwynn records, in *A Hundred Years of Catholic Emancipation*, that " Smith hurried back in jubilation with the news to Wiseman, who was utterly perplexed by such a manner of proclaiming truth."

How could Smith be so confident, the Cardinal argued, for Smith had to admit that he and Newman had barely referred to the matter.

He had no further information to give than that Newman had appeared in grey trousers at dinner !

" But I know the man," he declared, " and I know what it means."

For two months nothing occurred. Then several Anglo-Catholics made their vows, including some of Newman's friends, J. B. Dalgairns, W. G. Ward, the acknowledged leader of the party in Oxford, and Ambrose St John.

Edward Stanton, another friend, wrote to Newman of his intention to join the Catholic Church. Newman replied quickly : " Why should we not both be received together ? Father Dominic, the Passionist, comes here on the eighth to receive me. Come back on that day."

On October 9, 1845, Newman was received into the Roman Catholic Church by Father Dominic.

A fortnight later he was confirmed, and in October of the following year he went to Rome, was ordained priest and given the degree of D.D. by the Pope.

In 1847 he returned to England as an oratorian. He established the London Oratory, with Father Faber as its superior.

The Catholic Emancipation Act was passed in April, 1829, and on the 28th of that month the Catholic Peers took their seats in the House of Lords.

But matters did not go smoothly. There was considerable opposition to the Act in the country.

It was not, however, until an attempt was made to establish a hierarchy in England that active opposition really became serious.

Then came the dramatic announcement that Wiseman was to return to England as the head of the new Roman Catholic hierarchy with the title of Archbishop of Westminster.

On October 7, 1850, Wiseman sent out his famous pastoral letter. Immediately there was an outcry in the Press. An editorial in one newspaper went so far as to say :

It is no concern of ours whether Dr Wiseman chooses in Rome to be ranked with the *monsignori* of the capital. He is simply at Rome in the position of an English subject who has thought fit to enter the service of a foreign Power and accept its spurious dignities. . . .

We are informed by the " Official Gazette " of Rome that the Pope having been pleased to erect the city of Westminster into an archbishopric, and to appoint Dr Wiseman to that See, it is on this new-fangled Archbishop of Westminster, so appointed, that the rank of cardinal is so conferred.

It may be that the elevation of Dr Wiseman signified no more than if the Pope had been pleased to confer on the editor of the *Tablet* the rank and title of the Duke of Smithfield. But if this appointment be not intended as a clumsy joke, we confess we can only regard it as one of the grossest acts of folly and impertinence which the Court of Rome has ventured to commit since the Crown and people of England threw off its yoke.

On Sunday, October 27, Wiseman's pastoral was read in the Catholic churches. In the meantime the Press campaign was proceeding apace.

The storm was breaking; every one began to anticipate a recurrence of the Gordon riots ; Lord John Russell, the Prime Minister, replied to a letter by the Bishop of London in which he considered the " late aggression of the Pope upon our Protestantism " as " insolent and insidious," and shortly afterwards confirmed his views in a public speech at Guildhall.

But when the Chancellor of the Exchequer, at the Mansion House dinner, quoted the lines :

> Under our feet we'll stamp thy cardinal's hat,
> In spite of Pope or dignities of Church :

it was a signal for a general denunciation.

Coincident with Guy Fawkes Day, there was a gorgeous display of bonfires in which the Pope was burnt in effigy. At Salisbury they made the celebrations complete by including Wiseman and the twelve new Catholic bishops. The streets were crowded, and there were great scenes of enthusiasm when the effigies went up in flame and smoke. Any moment riots were expected.

Wiseman, still in Rome, knew nothing of what was going on, but when he was apprised of the opposition, he decided to come to London at once. He arrived on November 11 and made a public appearance outside St George's, Southwark. He was booed.

Then he wrote a manifesto to the English people. It appeared on November 19, and on the following day

was reproduced in full in the newspapers.   In a few days
30,000 copies were sold, and the newspaper which had
first opened the attack congratulated him " on his recovery of the use of the English language."

The next incident was the conversion of Archdeacon
Manning, of Chichester, and the consequent storm of
indignation in that See.

It was a long time before matters settled down.

XLVII

Garibaldi, Impetuous Wooer

EXILED from home, Giuseppe Garibaldi, afterwards the Italian Liberator, felt the need of a
friend. Though he was a ' pocket ' admiral in the navy
of the little Republic of Rio Grande do Sul, in South
America, he records :

> I felt quite alone in the world. I needed a human heart
> to love me, one that I could keep always near me.

The solution was a wife.

As he paced the ' quarter-deck ' of his flagship, a
top-sail schooner carrying seven guns, he raised his
telescope in a casual way and scanned the shore.

The telescope came to rest on the outlines of a pretty
villa, and as he watched he saw a dainty maiden sitting
beside the porch.

Garibaldi determined to investigate. He swung over
the wheel and the prow of the schooner was soon racing
through the waves. He stepped ashore, but the beautiful
girl had disappeared.

He wandered along the beach of Laguna, looking
right and left for the object of his search.

Suddenly a voice greeted him, and invited him to
" come in and have a cup of coffee." He went inside
and there, sitting at the table, was the maiden for whom
he was searching.

But Anita Riberas was already engaged to a man she
despised. Nevertheless she fell in love with Garibaldi

18   273

at first sight. Both were tongue-tied; neither could greet the other. At last Garibaldi blurted out, "You should be mine."

Garibaldi's ardour was irresistible. He was a handsome man; his exploits were known in many countries, although he had yet to gain the name of Liberator. The simple yet courageous Creole girl entirely lost her heart.

Says Trevelyan, his biographer:

> Such was the beginning of a love story which none of the world's most famous legends of love surpass in romance and beauty.

A week passed away, and then, at dead of night, Garibaldi broke into her house secretly and carried away his captive.

There is reason to believe that these 'cave-man' tactics were responsible for a tragedy. Perhaps there was a struggle, in which Anita's affianced husband was slain.

Nothing is known of the occurrence except those strange words of Garibaldi himself, which he uttered years later after the death of his wife:

> I had come upon a forbidden treasure, yet a treasure of great price. If guilt there was it was mine alone. And there was guilt.
>
> Two hearts were joined in an infinite love; but an innocent existence was shattered. She is dead; I am wretched; he is avenged, yes, avenged.

Anita was eighteen years of age, with a magnificent figure, a tender heart, and a courage equal to that of her husband.

"She had in her veins," continues Trevelyan, "the fighting blood of the race that ruled on horseback the deserts of Brazil, a Creole born, but with all the engaging manners of the señoritas of Old Spain. Her only uncontrolled passion was that love for which she risked her life, and lost it in the end."

Thus, through the fiercest of sea-fights, when shots swept the deck of Garibaldi's ship, she could never be prevailed upon to go below for safety.

Once, with a twelve-days-old baby, she escaped from the enemy by leaving her bed and fleeing on horseback through a forest infested with deadly snakes, while a tropical storm was raging.

And so she followed him through the next nine years of his life, " a friend, wife, fellow-soldier, page," often torn away from her husband, but finding him inevitably in the end.

Eventually she died in the arms of her husband, hunted to death by the Austrians.

That is the story of Garibaldi's love-romance. His achievements as Liberator of Italy show that he was equally determined in war as well as in love.

Garibaldi was born on July 4, 1807, in Nice. He was intended for the priesthood, but the family was a seafaring one.

There was no hope for it ; he would have to be a sailor.

Sailing on one of his father's trips he met a member of the patriotic league of ' Young Italy ' and joined the organization. He met Mazzini in Marseilles, who induced him to join in a plot against Charles Albert, the King of Piedmont.

A crowd of conspirators invaded the King's dominions, in the hope that the people would rise. The expedition failed, and Garibaldi, who was then in the navy as a spy, was sentenced to death.

He escaped, and, hunted by the police, he spent eleven days and nights in the mountains, and arrived home so tattered and torn that his mother did not know him. On the same evening he swam the river Var, then swollen by rains, and, arriving at Marseilles, he found notices asking for his apprehension.

He obtained a position as mate on the *Union*, and voyaged to and from the Black Sea. Once he jumped into the harbour at Marseilles to save a boy from drowning.

In 1836 he sailed for Rio de Janeiro. The Republic was at war with Brazil, and he threw in his lot with the smaller State.

After the birth of his first child he supported the family by teaching Italian, French, and mathematics in the colleges, but the Government of Montevideo, who had heard of his exploits against Brazil, enlisted his aid against the tyrant Rossa.

European countries had attempted to overthrow Rossa in vain, and it was a great triumph for Garibaldi when an English peer, Lord Howden, said in the House of Lords on July 10, 1849, that he was able to pay a tribute to " a person of great courage and military skill, who has a just claim on our sympathies, considering the unjustifiable intervention of the French and the recent and extraordinarily unnatural events that have taken place in Italy—I allude to General Garibaldi."

On April 15, 1848, sixty-three Italians sailed from Montevideo and, calling at the island of St Palo, learned of the Sicilian revolution and the Lombard war.

Garibaldi decided to land at Nice, and, with the addition of many volunteers, he went to the Royal camp and offered himself to the man who, years before, had condemned him to death, but was refused.

After the armistice of Salasco and the loss of Milan, Garibaldi carried on the war against the Austrians with his band of followers. When the Pope fled from Rome in November, 1848, Garibaldi and his two thousand followers took up his headquarters in Rieta in view of the attack on Rome by the King of Naples.

He was elected a member of the Assembly, and on February 9, 1849, his proposal of a republican form of government was passed.

Then came the attempts to restore the Pope on the part of the French, Austrians, Spaniards, and Neapolitans, but Garibaldi, with Mazzini, kept them at bay for months. The French army, almost at the gates of Rome, were routed. Then the Neapolitans were beaten.

Two months later the French made a further attack on Rome. Garibaldi, with a force half the strength of the enemy, was beaten and the French army marched into the Eternal City.

On the way to Ravenna, with the Austrians close upon their heels, Anita died in the arms of her husband in a peasant's hut. Fearing the Papal Government, the peasants buried her privately in a field, but her remains were discovered and those concerned were thrown into prison.

Garibaldi wandered for over a month in various disguises, was captured and thrown into prison at Genoa. Later he was released, and, being refused permission to land at Tunis, went to North America and obtained a job in a candle factory.

In 1860 he married again, but left his wife two days after the ceremony. Soon afterwards he was elected Deputy for Nice.

In the war between Austria and Prussia, in which Italy supported the latter, Garibaldi was put at the head of twenty battalions, and broke up the Austrian force at Lonato.

Garibaldi was wounded and laid aside for a time. During the rest of the war he had several brilliant engagements to his credit.

Garibaldi appeared unexpectedly at the Universal Peace Conference in Geneva, where he denounced the Papacy, and returned to Italy calling for volunteers to wipe out " the nest of vipers at Rome."

He was arrested and thrown into a fortress, but escaped.

He offered his services to France after the battle of Sedan, and was given command of 13,000 ill-equipped and ill-nourished troops, who fought many brilliant actions.

When, in 1864, Garibaldi visited England, no foreigner, up to that time, had received such an enthusiastic welcome.

Garibaldi died at Caprera in June, 1882.

XLVIII

ABRAHAM LINCOLN, THE EMANCIPATOR OF THE SLAVES

WHEN Abraham Lincoln heard that he had been nominated for the Presidency of the United States he said : " There is a little woman in Eighth Street who would like to hear about this."

This remark illustrates the characteristic simplicity of the man who had been born in a log cabin.

While the voting was going on, Lincoln and his wife waited at home through the strife of the election, calm and unemotional, content to allow his no-slavery policy to be judged by the people of the United States.

Then came news that he had been elected. A howl of fury went up from the Southern States, where immediately began talk about secession from the Union.

This meant open war, but in the meantime the Democratic *régime* continued, and the affairs of the Government were in the hands of men who openly supported the revolutionary elements.

They did not fail to take advantage of the few months of power. The Secretary of War, himself a Southerner, took care that the United States army was scattered all over the South, where it could be used at any moment to repel any movement from the North ; or, alternatively, when the days of the Government had expired, to separate the troops of Southern soil from their bases, should the Republicans wish to use them.

Moreover, steps were taken to have vast quantities of

arms and ammunition brought South. The Northern forts were practically emptied, and those of the slave States were full of munitions of war.

American warships were sent to all quarters of the globe, so that it would be impossible to call on them in the event of rebellion. The national finances, too, were deliberately involved, and the Secretary of the Treasury managed to clear the coffers of the Union.

The malcontents held their posts to the last minute, and then bolted, and when Lincoln was on his way to Washington to take up the Presidency there were threats that he would not be allowed to pass through Baltimore.

He reached Washington, however, and when the day came for him to make his maiden speech as President, and declare his policy, seven of the Southern States were already in rebellion, and a rival Government had been established in Montgomery.

Lincoln's speech was a model of moderation.

" Though passion may have strangled our relations," he said, " it must not break our bonds of affection."

Later he wrote a letter to the editor of the *New York Tribune*, in which he said :

> I would save the Union. . . . My paramount object is to save the Union, and not either to save or destroy slavery.
>
> If I could save the Union without freeing any slave, I would do it ; if I could save it by freeing all the slaves, I would do it ; and if I could do it by freeing some and leaving others alone, I would also do that.
>
> What I do about slavery and the coloured race I do because I believe it helps to save the Union.
>
> I shall do less whenever I believe that what I am doing hurts the cause.

" Save the Union . . . the Union before all else," was the keynote of his speech on the great open-air plat-

ABRAHAM LINCOLN
From a photograph taken at the White House
280

form in front of the Capitol, when he made his first address as President.

Then he groped for the hat which he had mislaid. The man who held it, and returned it to the new President, was Douglas, the retiring President, who had been his bitterest enemy.

" Mr President, may I have the honour of shaking hands with you," he said, " and will you accept an old opponent's word that we are all at one in supporting you to uphold the Constitution ? "

While Lincoln was forming his Cabinet seven Southern States declared themselves out of the Union, assembled their Parliament at Montgomery, and passed a bill organizing an army. But Lincoln gave no sign ; he was determined not to be frightened into making the first blow.

Then when two men were sent to Washington by the Southern States to negotiate a treaty Lincoln refused to see them, but, with dry humour, ordered that they should each be given a copy of his inaugural speech, so that they should not be under any misapprehension as to his policy.

In the meantime Lincoln was having trouble with a Cabinet of divergent views. He removed his first War Secretary on finding that he was receiving bribes from people anxious for office ; his second War Secretary was reprimanded because of his open boast that he could rule Lincoln. Then the two became fast friends.

There were other quarrels in the Cabinet, and the situation was by no means pleasant when Civil War began by the Confederates firing upon Fort Sumter in Charleston Harbour, South Carolina, where a small Government garrison was on the point of running short of supplies.

During the war, Lincoln surmounted each crisis with unflinching courage, patience, and always with gentleness.

Over the fallen of Gettysburg he said :

Fourscore and seven years ago our fathers brought forth on this continent a new nation, conceived in liberty, and dedicated to the proposition that all men are created equal. Now we are engaged in a great civil war, testing whether that nation or any other nation so conceived and so dedicated can long endure. We are met on a great battlefield of war. We have come to dedicate a portion of that field as a final resting-place for those who have given their lives, that the nation might live. It is altogether fitting and proper that we should do this.

But in a larger sense we cannot dedicate, we cannot consecrate, we cannot hallow this ground. The brave men, living and dead, who struggled here have consecrated here far above our power to add or detract. The world will little note, nor long remember, what we say here, but it can never forget what they did here.

It is for us, the living, rather to be dedicated here to the unfinished work which they who fought here have thus far so nobly advanced.

It is rather for us to be here dedicated to the great task remaining before us—that from these honoured dead we take increased devotion to that cause for which they gave the last full measure of devotion ; that we here highly resolve that these dead shall not have died in vain ; that this nation, under God, shall have a new birth of freedom ; and that government of the people by the people for the people, shall not perish from the earth.

Abraham Lincoln was born on February 12, 1809, in a one-roomed log cabin in Kentucky. His parents were poor settlers, and their home was far from any other habitation.

In the intense silence of the Kentucky backwoods Lincoln first learned his alphabet from his mother, and when in his seventh year went to a little log school-house that had just been established near by.

Then the family went to Indiana, and when Abraham was nine his mother died, and he had to help to dig the grave. He studied the life of Washington, and read many famous works.   At the age of nineteen he obtained a job on a river-boat, and on his voyages down the Mississippi made a close study of slavery.   He was particularly affected by the flogging of female slaves.

He opened a store, progressed, and then decided to stand for the Legislature.   He failed to gain election, but two years later was successful.   In 1837 he started in practice as a lawyer at Springfield, Illinois.

It was from this small town that he made his journey to the White House at Washington.

XLIX

KARL MARX, VISIONARY

THERE is a grave in Highgate Cemetery which is visited by scores of people who make a yearly pilgrimage there to pay their respects to a man who was the originator of theories which led to the introduction of an important force into world-politics.

The inscription on the tomb records the death of four people, one of whom is Karl Marx. The others are his wife, their grandson, Henry Longuet, and their servant, Helen Dernuth.

To understand the principles of Marx and the place which his followers have assigned to him in history, it is necessary only to refer to the oration of Marx's companion and friend, Friedrich Engels, delivered on the occasion of the interment of the philosopher's remains.

It was as follows :

> The loss which his death has inflicted upon the fighting proletariat in Europe and America, and upon the science of history, is immeasurable. The gaps that will be made by the death of this titan will soon be felt. . . .
>
> Before all else, Marx was a revolutionist. To collaborate in one way or another in the overthrow of capitalist society and of the State institutions created by that society ; to collaborate in the freeing of the modern proletariat, which he was the first to inspire with a consciousness of its needs, with a knowledge of the conditions requisite for its emancipation—this was his true mission in life. Fighting was his natural element. Few men ever fought with so much passion, tenacity, and success. . . .
>
> Had Marx done nothing but found the International, that was an achievement of which he might well have been proud.

Since Russia became Communist, attempts have been made to have Marx's remains removed to Russia without avail, and the grave is kept tidy by a few Germans, who have raised a fund for the purpose.

If Marx's career be studied without prejudice, it is full of interest and not without pathetic incident. Like so many other men who have made a mark in history, he suffered from ill-health. Liver trouble, considered a family disease, caused him to fear cancer of the liver. It was this which gave him such a pronounced inferiority complex.

Although his family were Protestants, they were of Jewish extraction. He had been born a Jew and could never forget it ; he despised Judaism. " What is the mundane cult of the Jews ? " he asked, and his own reply was " Huckstering." " What is the Jews' mundane god ?—Money." And so, prejudiced against his own race, he had an additional reason for hiding himself — physically speaking — from the eyes of the world.

Perhaps the inferiority complex did not appear until later years, for there is evidence that he could be assertive as a young man.

There is, for instance, the story of his " cave-man " wooing of Jenny von Westphalen. Jenny was of high birth, the daughter of an important Government official, and the belle of Trèves. Marx knew that there were many far more presentable than he, but, setting aside his self-consciousness, he succeeded against any number of suitors.

When the parents on both sides objected, Marx was not dismayed. He and Jenny became engaged, and eventually the parental blessing was given. This achievement filled Marx with confidence and a determination to excel in his studies at the University. Jenny was the lineal descendant of the Earl of Argyll, who was beheaded under James II.

All through life he was proud of his wife, and once, after visiting his birthplace, he wrote to her :

> Almost every one I meet asks me for news of " the prettiest girl in Trèves," for tidings of " the queen of the ballroom." It cannot but tickle a man to find that in the fancy of a whole township his wife is enshrined as " fairy Princess."

In 1836 Marx went to Berlin University and chose jurisprudence as a special study, although he was equally interested in history and philosophy.

At the University he developed Radical views and, instead of taking his degrees, he joined the staff of the *Rheinische Zeitung*, a Radical organ. In the autumn of 1843 he went to Paris to study Socialism, and it was there that he met Friedrich Engels, the two collaborating in literary work.

They went to Brussels together and came into close contact with the Socialist working-class movement, founded a German workers' society, acquired a local German weekly, and, finally, joined a Communistic society of German workers, the " League of the Just," a secret society with branches in London, Paris, Brussels, and a number of Swiss towns. In connexion with this society, Marx and Engels wrote their pamphlet, *Manifest der Kommunisten*, a history of the working-class movement and an explanation of the Communist standpoint.

In February, 1848, the Revolution broke out in France, and after spending a short time there, Marx and Engels went to Cologne and founded a newspaper which they described as " an organ of democracy." It was published daily, and Marx was the editor. When the Prussian National Assembly was dissolved in the same year, Marx advocated the non-payment of taxes and armed resistance.

Marx's newspaper was suspended, a state of siege was declared at Cologne, and Marx was brought to trial for high treason. He was acquitted, but soon expelled from Prussian territory.

He went to France, but was given the alternative of leaving the country or living in a provincial town. He chose the former and came to England, where he remained to the end of his life.

In London he lived in poverty in small rooms in Soho, and all his children who were born during this time died in infancy. At last he obtained work for the *New York Tribune*, and was paid a guinea each for his contributions.

In 1859 he denounced the Franco-Austrian war, and declared it to be a Franco-Russian intrigue ; and in the same year he sat down to write his famous work, *Das Kapital*, which was eventually published in 1867.

Meantime the International Working Men's Association was inaugurated in London, and although Marx was not the head in name he was actually the inspiring genius.

All its literature was written by Marx. He was more a theorist than an agitator, and often restrained the extremists of the party, adopting a middle course of compromise which satisfied in the end both right and left.

It was probably Michael Bakunin who eventually brought about the fall of the International. Bakunin was a Russian of good family, with distinctly anarchistic views. He had been arrested in 1844 in Saxony after the Dresden rising, and condemned to death. Instead of being executed he was handed over to the Austrians, tried once more, and sentenced to death. Again he escaped the death penalty by being handed over to Russia, imprisoned in the fortress of St Peter and St Paul, and afterwards sent to Siberia. He escaped, and reached London in 1861, and had an interview with Marx, at which the two men appear to have adjusted their earlier differences.

Bakunin was head of the International Alliance of the Socialist Democracy, which Marx regarded as a rival of the International. Marx described the programme of Bakunin as " an olla podrida of worn-out commonplaces, thoughtless chatter ; a rose-garland of empty notions and insipid improvization."

When Bakunin became a member of the International there was not room for two men of such outstanding characteristics, and Marx decided to get rid of him.

The methods that Marx employed to do this were reprehensible. He declared that Bakunin had embezzled money intended for propaganda purposes, although there was not a word of truth in it. Many other accusations were made, and the crisis came following the breakdown of the Paris Commune in 1871.

A congress of the International was held at The Hague, and the seat of the General Council was moved from London to New York, but it was not long before the whole thing collapsed, and in 1876 the International was dissolved at a conference in Philadelphia.

By reason of his unjustifiable attacks on Bakunin, Marx had almost become a discredited man in the Socialist movement. He returned to his scientific work and his attempts to send the second and third volumes of *Das Kapital* to the press, but he became very depressed, mainly because he lacked money.

It was in this connexion that Engels came to his rescue. Asked how much he required to pay off his debts, Marx replied by letter :

> I am quite overcome by your extreme kindness. My wife and I have gone into the figures together, and we find that the amount of the debts is much larger than I had supposed—£210 (of which about £75 are for the pawnshop and interest).

Engels succeeded in disposing of his business interests, paid off Marx's debts, and went to live near him.

In 1873 onwards, Marx suffered from bad headaches : his liver trouble recurred. With Engel's help he went to Karlsbad in 1874, 1875, and 1876, and although he derived a certain amount of temporary benefit, he became worse year by year. The collapse of the International was a great blow ; *Das Kapital* had not reached his expectations, while a Social-Democratic movement in Germany was started without his advice.

Then his wife fell ill and died, while Marx was suffering from bronchitis and pleurisy. Two years later his favourite daughter died, and three months afterwards Marx himself was dead.

At his funeral the only persons present were Engels and half a dozen other friends.

19

L

" THE LADY OF THE LAMP "

> Are there no devoted women amongst us, able and willing
> to go forth to minister to the sick and suffering soldiers of the
> East ?

WHEN Russell, the war correspondent of *The Times*,
wrote this phrase in his dispatch to his newspaper,
the Rt. Hon. Sidney Herbert, War Minister, hoped—and
yet feared—that it might catch the eyes of Florence
Nightingale.

He feared because he knew her personally and was
aware that she had already suffered two nervous break-
downs as a result of her hospital work in this country.
Would such an arduous task as taking over complete
charge of the hospital work in the Crimea be too much
for her ?

The situation in the East was deplorable.

> When I was looking at the wounded men going off to-day,
> I could not see an English ambulance [wrote Russell]. Our
> men were sent to the sea, three miles distant, on jolting arabas
> or tedious litters. The French had well-appointed covered
> hospital vans . . . and their wounded were sent in much
> greater comfort than our poor fellows.
>
> Are none of the daughters of England, at this extreme hour
> of need, ready for such a work of mercy . . . ?
>
> Must we fall so far below the French in self-sacrifice and
> devotedness, in a work which Christ so signally blesses as done
> unto Himself ?

That appeal brought hundreds of women to the War
Office, but they had received no training ; they knew

nothing of hospital duty or organization. There was, in 1854, hardly a nurse capable of being entrusted even with a cottage hospital.

In the opinion of Sidney Herbert there was only one, Florence Nightingale. Dare he write to her to ask her to take on the gigantic task?

He wrote to her, but while he was doing this Florence Nightingale was writing to him offering her services. Their letters crossed.

A week later Florence Nightingale, with her first batch of thirty-eight nurses, left London. Another fortnight and they were at Scutari and had taken up their quarters in the barrack hospital.

The wounded soldiers were starving ; there were no vessels for water or utensils of any kind. There were no hospital clothes, soap, or towels. The men lay in their uniforms, stiff with blood and covered with filth and vermin.

The hospital was infested with rats that ventured close to the wounded soldiers and drew blood with their teeth. One of the first things that Florence Nightingale did as she entered the hospital was to frighten away a rat from above a bed.

On the day after the nurses arrived the Battle of Inkerman was fought, so that before she could clear up the mess at the hospital a new lot of wounded began to come in to add to Florence Nightingale's difficulties.

Many of the wounded had fever or cholera ; they took up every inch of space in the vast hospital. Many died on the ground outside.

It appeared a hopeless situation. Florence Nightingale worked twenty hours a day ushering in and apportioning places to the broken men. Nurses were not allowed to malinger. She insisted upon cleanliness everywhere, and the orderlies whose duty it was to inspect the wards realized that Miss Nightingale had a knack of finding things out, and did not slacken at their work.

They soon did more for her than their official duties demanded.

> Never [she wrote afterwards] came from any one of them one word or one look which a gentleman would not have used.
>
> The tears come into my eyes as I think how, amidst loathsome scenes of disease and death, there arose above it all the innate dignity, gentleness, and chivalry of the men, shining in the midst of what must be considered as the lowest sinks of human misery, and preventing instinctively the use of one expression which would distress a gentlewoman.

It was not only the hospital that became efficient; Government contractors were compelled to mend their ways and deliver their goods punctually. A man who had the contract for washing was dispensed with because of his irregularity, and Florence Nightingale set up a laundry herself.

When the war settled down to the siege of Sebastopol, frostbite caused more trouble than wounds. The cholera was of the worst type, and a man attacked was dead in five hours.

There were almost as many stretchers carrying out the dead as there were stretchers bringing in the sick. The death-rate was 60 per cent.

Night after night, when the orderlies had retired, fagged out, Florence Nightingale would go around the endless galleries with her lamp to ascertain the condition of her patients, smoothing a pillow or gently relieving a delirious man.

In May, 1855, the situation at Scutari had so far improved that Florence Nightingale was able to take a journey to the seat of war.

She sailed up the Bosphorus to Balaklava and visited

the hospitals there, and then took a ride to Sebastopol to watch the siege operations. She insisted upon entering the trenches, despite the artillery fire.

Towards the end of the summer peace was in sight. Already Queen Victoria was considering how the nation could best show its gratitude to Florence Nightingale. She wrote to her War Minister, and he replied :

> MADAM—There is but one testimonial which would be accepted by Miss Nightingale. The one wish of her heart has long been to found a hospital in London and to work it on her own system of unpaid nursing ; and I have suggested to all who have asked for my advice in this matter to pay any sums that they may feel disposed to give, or that they may be able to collect, into Messrs Coutts' Bank, where a subscription list for the purpose is about to be opened, to be called the Nightingale Hospital Fund—the sum subscribed to be presented to her on her return home, which will enable her to carry out her object regarding the reform of the nursing system of England.

The scheme was inaugurated in the following November, and at the meeting Sidney Herbert repeated the words of a wounded soldier brought back to health in Scutari hospital :

> She would speak to one and another and nod and smile to many more ; but she could not do it to all, you know, for we lay there by hundreds. But we could kiss her shadow as it fell, and lay our heads on the pillow again content.

The subscriptions came in so fast that Miss Nightingale had to stop them. Then she returned to the Crimea, and nursed the wounded that still remained and the sick men in the army of occupation.

While there she received the following letter from Queen Victoria :

> DEAR MISS NIGHTINGALE—You are, I know, well aware of the high sense I entertain of the Christian devotion which you have displayed during this great and bloody war, and I need

hardly repeat to you how warm my admiration is for your
services, which are fully equal to those of my dear and brave
soldiers, whose sufferings you have had the privilege of relieving
in so merciful a manner.

I am, however, anxious of marking my feelings in a manner
which I trust will be agreeable to you, and therefore send you
with this letter a brooch, the form and emblems of which commemorate your great and blessed work, and which I hope you
will wear as a mark of the high approbation of your Sovereign.

It will be a great satisfaction to me, when you return at last
to these shores, to make the acquaintance of one who had set so
bright an example to your sex.   And with every prayer for the
preservation of your valuable health, believe me, always your
sincerely,   VICTORIA R.

It was expected that there would be a great demonstration when Florence Nightingale returned to England,
but she declined to be brought home by a battleship,
and travelled under an assumed name to England.

It is said that she entered the back door of her house
at Lea Hurst to avoid publicity.

She rested for a time, hoping that her health would
return, and that she would be able to undertake active
work in connexion with the new nursing movement,
but her strength would not allow this, and, greatly dis-
appointed, she had to give up the idea.

Nevertheless, the scheme went on, while she lived as a
recluse and wrote a number of books, such as *Notes on
Hospitals*, and *Notes on Nursing*, and pamphlets.

Toward the end of her life she was not in a position
to resist the honours which fell upon her.   Already she
had received the Red Cross from Queen Victoria, and
on her eighty-fourth birthday, May 12, 1904, she was
made a Lady of Grace of the Order of St John of Jerusalem by King Edward, and three years later received
the Order of Merit.

She was the first woman to be awarded the Order of

Merit, but the greatest tribute to her memory is the testimony contained in the simple phrase, " The Lady of the Lamp." In 1908 she received the freedom of the City of London.

Florence Nightingale, who was the second daughter of William Edward Nightingale, of Tapton, Derbyshire, entered the Deaconess Hospital at Kaiserswerth, on the Rhine, just before she was thirty.

Here she learned discipline, so that she was to write afterwards :

> Three-fourths of the whole mischief in women's lives arises from their excepting themselves from the rules of training considered needful for men. I would say to all young ladies who are called to any vocation : " Qualify yourselves for it as a man does for his work."

She died on August 13, 1910, and was buried at East Wellow, Hampshire.

LI

Louis Pasteur, who believed that all was Miracle

IT was while on a visit to a brewery that Louis Pasteur made a discovery which led to a revolution in chemical and biological science.

He found that globules from sound beer were nearly spherical, those from sour beer elongated.

At this time the phenomena of fermentation was a mystery. No one had been able to explain its cause with any certainty.

Theories had been advanced, but all had been discredited.

Following his visit to the brewery Pasteur began his tests. He eventually discovered that fermentation was due to the presence and growth of minute organisms. If these organisms were excluded no change occurred. Milk would keep permanently fresh, brewers' wort would remain unchanged.

But having discovered this, Pasteur was faced with other problems :

> Why did beer or milk become sour when exposed to the air ?
> Whence came these invisible organisms ?
> Did they come from the atmosphere, or were they generated in the liquid ?

These questions led to a controversy waged by scientists all over the world.

Pasteur maintained that they were atmospheric

germs, and that it was possible to exclude them. By experiments designed to keep the liquid from contact with the air he proved his case.

In the interior of the grape, he said, there were no germs, and if the fruit were kept from damage so that no air could get inside, the grape would remain fresh indefinitely.

The same process applied to wounds of animals. When exposed to the air the wound became infected.

These discoveries revolutionized the brewing and wine-making industries, and Pasteur was the recipient of honours from many countries.

He was given an important post in Paris, where he was allowed to continue his researches.

He now proposed, on the same lines, to prevent and cure disease due to germs. Many of his friends declared that he could never hope to achieve this.

He laughed at their criticism, and replied : " Work, work, always."

The great test was soon to come.

An epidemic among silkworms had ruined the silk industry of France. Pasteur was asked to undertake an investigation. He went to one of the chief centres of silk production.

He had never before seen a silkworm, and was dubious about carrying out the researches.

Three months afterwards—September, 1865—he had reached the end of his experiments and was able to publish the result. He had found the parasite that preyed on the worm.

The silk trade of France was saved by the elimination of the disease. It has been said that Pasteur's work in this sphere alone saved enough to pay the whole in-demnity of the Franco-Prussian War.

" There is no greater charm for the investigator than

to make new discoveries," was the remark of the biologist when he had achieved this remarkable result. " But," he added, " his pleasure is heightened when he sees that they have a direct application to practical life."

When Pasteur had concluded his researches into the disease of silkworms he turned his attention to the diseases in fowls caused by microbes. Meanwhile he had discovered that a microbe was at the bottom of the animal disease known as anthrax. This, too, was also a disease of human beings, and it was while he was carrying out his experiments in this direction, that the first discovery was made that certain diseases in men were also due to microbes.

Pasteur found that the effect of microbes could be modified, so that when animals were vaccinated with weak strains they could be protected subsequently from infection with virulent strains.

Many years before, Jenner had done this in connexion with small-pox without, however, understanding the facts.

In course of time, Pasteur was able to protect animals from anthrax disease, and he thus performed a greater service to humanity than was the case even with the silk industry.

Having reached the stage of human disease, he tackled hydrophobia. He found a method of curing this disease by inoculation. But he never found the microbe ; it is so minute that the microscope cannot discover it.

His first experiment was on a shepherd boy who had been bitten by a wolf.

The treatment of hydrophobia had progressed to such an extent by 1895, the year of Pasteur's death, that 122 cases were treated in that year without a single death.

Louis Pasteur, who may be described as the founder of preventive medicine, was born at Dôle, France, on December 27, 1822. He studied at Besançon and afterwards in Paris, where he soon came under the influence of the leading chemist of the day.

While he was studying, he earned his own living by teaching in the universities. He was forty-four when he became Professor of Chemistry at the Sorbonne.

About that time there was considerable controversy on the question of spontaneous generation. Pasteur held the opinion that life could not appear in vessels from which it had been excluded, or in any in which previous life had been destroyed by heat.

At the time it was supposed that Pasteur had finally disposed of the argument, but since his day it has been proved that he was wrong.

However, if this controversy did nothing more than make Pasteur more enthusiastic in his researches, it resulted in a great benefit to humanity.

Pasteur was sixty-three when the French provided him with an institute which, named after him, is one of the world-centres for the study, cure, and the prevention of disease. From the Pasteur Institute came the anti-toxin for diphtheria. Among the famous men who were pupils of Pasteur were Lister, the Englishman (afterwards Lord Lister), and Koch, the German.

To Pasteur, the pioneer, is due the success of Lord Lister in surgery.

Without the researches of the great French chemist, Lister, the " Saviour of Millions of Lives," would have been unable to achieve his remarkable successes in the fight against infectious disease.

In 1874 he wrote to Pasteur :

> Allow me to take this opportunity to tender you my most cordial thanks for having, by your brilliant researches, demonstrated to me the truth of the germ theory of putrefaction, and thus furnished me with the principles upon which alone the antiseptic system can be carried out.

Pasteur had accomplished a great deal of spade work, but few had seen its significance. In Pasteur's time, the death-rate in cases of amputation was 60 per cent. or more. When Lister introduced carbolic acid in 1868, the deaths from amputation were reduced to 20 per cent. Lister was quick to realize that even a pin-point can carry a fatal injury.

At Munich hospital, gangrene followed in 80 per cent. of the amputation cases until Listerism was adopted.

Under the new *régime* gangrene was almost negligible. All this success was undoubtedly based upon Pasteur's discovery of diseased germs.

Pasteur died on September 28, 1895, and was buried in a special chapel under the Pasteur Institute. His favourite motto was, " One must keep working," and he lived up to this all his life. He was a devout Catholic, and his favourite expression in philosophy was, " All is miracle."